CW00459086

Whatever
Name
or
Creed

Hymns and Songs

by

Andrew Pratt

Stainer & Bell

First published in 2002 by
Stainer & Bell Limited, PO Box 110, Victoria House, 23 Gruneisen Road,
London N3 1DZ, England.

All rights reserved. This book is copyright under the Berne Convention. It is fully protected by the
British Copyright, Designs and Patents Act 1988. No part of the work may be reproduced, stored in
a retrieval system, or transmitted in any form by any means, electronic, photocopying or otherwise
without the prior permission of Stainer & Bell Ltd unless otherwise stated below.

The copyright in the compilation, prefatory material, notes, typography and music setting of this
volume vests in Stainer & Bell Ltd.

The copyright in the individual music of hymns (except where the copyright is credited to
third parties) and the copyright in the individual hymn texts vests in Stainer & Bell Ltd. For
permission to reproduce any text or tune owned by Stainer & Bell Ltd, application should be made
to Hope Publishing Company, 380 South Main Place, Carol Stream, Illinois 60188 for the USA
and Canada and Stainer & Bell Ltd for all other territories.

The tunes by Peter Cutts are owned for the USA and Canada by Hope Publishing Company
(see above).

The texts of Andrew Pratt may also as at the date of publication be copied by those holding a
current Church Copyright Licensing Ltd licence provided the items copied are included on
their returns.

Cover illustration: Driftwood and acrylic on paper by Jonathan Pratt (1976–1999)

British Library Cataloguing-in-Publication Data
A catalogue record of this book is available from the British Library

ISBN: 0 85249 874 8

This book is available in the USA and Canada through Hope Publishing Company,
380 South Main Place, Carol Stream, Illinois 60188, USA

Printed in Great Britain by Caligraving Ltd, Thetford

Contents

Introduction

It is a great delight to write the introduction for *Whatever Name or Creed*. Andrew Pratt is one of our foremost contemporary hymn-writers. In his work he encourages people to relate to their own community, to the wider society and to our global situation. He encapsulates the core of life with the essence of what we should be about in our lives – whether within or without the church.

> Christ, we do not recognise
> your face in all the world...
>
> Neither do we recognise
> love longs to meet that need. (5)

With lines like these, Andrew brings us into the twenty-first century, which is where we need to be for the starting-point of our living and worshipping.

Many people who have an integral role in the life of the church find themselves increasingly marginalised within it, because of their understanding of life and of how they empathise with society. This hymn collection will encourage many of our dedicated women and men to remain where they are and to proceed on their pilgrim journey. Also, it will help many people who are wanting to discover new and fresh ways of being church with the world. 'Why are we so lost, forsaken? Kindle, God, some expectation.' (8)

There is often the time when Christians talk of being free, yet so often we are constrained by a misinterpretation of Christianity or convention. We are reminded constantly that our 'God of awe and wonder speaks through... rainbow, stars or thunder...' (18)

This is a wide-ranging and down-to-earth collection that will help people to bring in the Kingdom where it should be, here on earth. Andrew writes of his hymn *This love, this life, this enterprise* that 'It is in our actions that God is made present'. In verse two we sing:

> Our practical adventure here
> involves both urgency and care;
> compelled by shared humanity
> to offer love, set people free. (72)

In another hymn, we reflect on the enigmatic, scandalous love of God, as demonstrated by Jesus's concern for the outcast:

> Outrageous love that dares to breach
> the dam of our desire...

Enigma: friend, Messiah, God;
while hypocrites despair
you die to love discarded souls;
enable our repair. (40)

We are also there for the wedding of Andrew's niece, Emma Daniels, to Jamie Burstow:

Let us join their celebration:
pray for all they wish to share;
love, and loving ever after,
understanding, strength to care. (42)

Relations and friends who have long given up on regular attendance at worship will find in these writings aspects of love and life that the church needs to (re)discover. These hymns will speak to many people across the age-ranges who have forsaken the church because they consider it has no relevance to their lives. We are given opportunities to embark upon a greater appreciation of Celtic spirituality, to explore the incarnation, to be 'earthed' in the life of a local church through the dedication of new lighting, and to be inspired by the Christmas lights of a small town.

An increasing number of people appreciate the growing need to enhance their understanding of our faith communities. There is a desperate need to recognise the common features that bind together the major world religions, and we are helped to do this in a verse such as the following:

O Source of many cultures,
of lives, beliefs and faith;
you brought us all together
to share one world in space; (62)

Many aspects of life are reflected in this fine collection. This is what is needed for today's society. There are ministers, pastoral carers, people searching and seeking, who need to find the hymns and the reflections that will enable them to participate effectively in births, baptisms, marriages, deaths and new beginnings – and we should sing about those times as well. It is with great joy that one goes on discovering the treasures in this hymn-feast.

So, tell people all about these hymns and songs, and welcome them into your worship. They are not only for minority groups to enjoy, but also for worshipping people of all faith-understandings to sing, to read, to be challenged by and, by them, to be encouraged to go out and love the dispossessed, the sad, the bewildered, the joyful, the searchers, the creationists and the conservationists, along with those people who are not accepted because of who and where they are.

Geoffrey Duncan
April 2002

Preface

'The measure of our grief at missing those we love is the measure of what we have been given through them.'   Revd David Cook, Chaplain, Cranbrook School, Kent, England

Hymns have to stand alone, to be sung and understood without additional comment or explanation. Yet people have commented to me that they are interested in the background of individual texts. They want to know how and why they were written.

Some two years after the publication of my first collection of texts, *Blinded by the Dazzle* (Stainer & Bell, 1997), my son was killed in an accident. He was twenty-two years old and a university student. The experience of his death has had an incalculable effect on me. I have in no way lost my faith but it has changed radically. An exploration of the beliefs of others has led me to a practical, working acknowledgement that they are every bit as valid as my own. I have held fast to much but also gained immeasurably.

What is the nature of this changed faith?

Every day there is more that I do not know, more of which I'm less sure. A breeze can ripple a reflection. When the water settles again, clouds have moved, the perspective is different. Equally, my faith can alter. The change is often gradual, sometimes traumatic. I have found religious faith to be dynamic rather than static. To that extent I am agnostic. Things which I thought were neatly tied up have a habit of unravelling. There is more mystery. That is helpful, as I hope it will prevent me from making bold statements that are then overturned when I'm confronted by a different perspective or a new discovery.

I'm Methodist by choice. While this denomination is not unique, Methodism, at its best, has an openness to religious exploration bonded to a strong social conscience, a care for people and a love of hymnody. Hymns are still vehicles for individual personal devotion, to be read rather than sung, as well as a means for congregational song.

I am Christian because I still believe that Jesus's words and actions have something relevant and important to say about our living human life fully, compassionately, rightly and well with each other. The metaphor of incarnation has not lost its currency.

I am religious because, on the one hand, I believe that there is 'something' more than this cosmos of which we have immediate sensory experience. I have an open mind as to the 'something', and the term 'god' is not always helpful as it brings with it so much baggage. On the other hand, I cannot believe that any single religion has the monopoly of understanding, practice or belief in relation to this ground of being.

The consequence for this collection is a variety of theme and an exploration of subject-matter. It also provides a hint to my personal religious pilgrimage during the last few years. I have been challenged to look at the claims of faiths other than Christianity, including those outside the mainstream and, in their light, to try to make sense of my own beliefs and understanding of the cosmos, and who or what lies behind it. The chronological arrangement of texts reflects this, but also shows how faith develops through twists and turns. Places and experiences are revisited and still found helpful.

Hymnody has long since ceased to be simply 'the praise of God sung'. Some of my new hymns and songs are descriptive of God or God's people, some are in the form of conversations with the deity. All employ words that I have used, or would imagine myself using, in the circumstances to which the texts relate. This often gives an indication as to their source of inspiration. Many of the items included have been written in response to specific situations or events. Since *Blinded by the Dazzle* I have written hymns of an orthodox Christian nature, for corporate worship, and items for the individual. There are also texts which explore how far we can go in giving expression to Christian concepts while using everyday language. It has been equally important to me to raise questions of doubt and religious uncertainty in my writing. Doubt does not undermine faith but opens windows on new possibilities.

Those who wish to worship with people of other faiths will find material here. The words are written from a Christian perspective, which is my own. It is for non-Christians to judge whether I have provided anything of value for them. I hope these hymns will offer a challenge to Christians and non-Christians alike as to what we sing when those of different faiths come together for worship. That we should is, for me, beyond the point of dispute. As we do we will rehearse with each other similar issues to those which exercised Christian ecumenists in the last century. I am even more firmly convinced of the need for this broader ecumenism since the destruction of the World Trade Center in New York on 11 September 2001, and the religious stereotyping and hatred which has been whipped up in its wake.

We must find ways of sharing in our common humanity *whatever name or creed* we bear.

Andrew Pratt
May 2002

Acknowledgements

Jackie, my wife, has continued to be unfailingly patient with my passion for hymnody and religious exploration. We have shared so much pain and joy, and this book would not have come to fruition without her. I am also grateful to Damian Boddy who has helped me with the selection and transcription of tunes, and Janet Wootton who has made helpful suggestions relating to the editing of texts.

This book is dedicated, with gratitude,
to Elizabeth Daniels, my mother-in-law.

Hymns and Songs

All your world of haste and hurry
leaves me standing, frozen, cold;
what is life that has no future?
What is love that has no hold?

All is bleak and unforgiving:
hope extinguished, filled with fear;
now the light is quickly fading
shadows make my way unclear.

Lost in silent desperation,
calling out, my voice unheard;
can you sense my hope's extinction,
speak a reassuring word?

Can you bring a word to save me
from a life that's worse than death;
can you offer love to raise me
from this mire of helplessness?

Saviour hear my plea, and promise
in this season's hopelessness,
never to deride or pity,
always to be near to bless;

Lift me from my life of sorrow,
from the depths of dark despair;
let me see a bright tomorrow,
let me taste the cool clear air.

Let me ride the wings of morning,
let me praise each day begun,
let me live with joy and gladness
to the setting of the sun!

© 2000 Stainer & Bell Ltd

Metre: 8.7.8.7. Trochaic

Suggested Tunes: MERTON and WELLESLEY

Written 1994

The last three verses could be replaced with this verse:

Stranded in a vale of sorrow,
in the darkness, damned, bereft;
Saviour hear my plea and hold me
through this season's dark distress.

This text pleads for a better understanding of depression, and in particular that sense of futility depressed people often experience amid the hectic pace of our busy and apparently fulfilled lives. The theme was suggested to me by Jackie, my wife.

Riots rout the city's beauty,
anger flares and blood runs free;
in the shadows, quietly weeping,
is God watching, will God see?

If God sees what can be offered?
Platitudes of mindless hope?
Is God so detached, uncaring,
leaving us alone to cope?

This is not what had been promised,
streets of anger, greed born towers:
but, as pavements burn our footsteps,
we belong, for these are ours.

Will God share our tortured anguish,
enter into our distress;
walk the barren city with us,
know its caustic hopelessness?

In unquiet imagination
we can see our dreams fulfilled.
God, hung on a cross, is watching,
God, in desolation skilled.

© 1995 Stainer & Bell Ltd

Written 1995

Metre: 8.7.8.7. Trochaic

Suggested Tunes: SHIPSTON and BENG-LI

First published in 'Worship Live' Volume 1 No. 2. A reflection on the bleaker side of city life in the 1980s and 90s (... and now?), and God's incarnate presence. There is also an implicit questioning of the rightness of the Capitalism into which we, in the West, are bound.

3 How we insulate ourselves from feeling

CHADWICK

Peter Cutts (1937–)

How we in - su - late our - selves from feel - ing, how we hide,___ ___ a - void - ing oth - ers' sight;___ safe, co - cooned, our deep re - serve con - -ceal - ing strength that would sus - tain us in this plight.

© 1989 Stainer & Bell Ltd for the world except USA and Canada

How we insulate ourselves from feeling,
how we hide, avoiding others' sight;
safe, cocooned, our deep reserve concealing
strength that would sustain us in this plight.

Death we face in chaos and disorder,
pain we suffer, nothing could assuage;
yet God's love is deeper than disaster
reaching from the past beyond this age.

Close to God new order stems from chaos,
purpose finds a place within this life,
chance, as much as certainty, informs us,
strong in love we answer to the strife.

© 2000 Stainer & Bell Ltd

Metre: 10.9.10.9.

Written 31 December 1996

Inspired by 'Shadowlands' – a film about the writer C. S. Lewis. Humanly, we shield ourselves from the pain associated with grief, but in consequence the wound may fester or remain unhealed.

4 An enigmatic preacher

POLDHU

Peter Cutts (1937–)

An en - ig - ma - tic preach - er, a mys - tic or a rogue? He drew the peo - ple near to him a - long the Jor - dan road.

© 1985 Stainer & Bell Ltd for the world except USA and Canada

A fiery, forceful prophet
who preached the word of God
to Pharisee and Sadduccee
and others time forgot.

He called them to repentance,
baptised, and then prepared
those folk to hear demanding news
that Jesus came to share.

He threatened vested interests,
the hypocrites exposed;
condemned to face an unjust death
by powers that he opposed.

Imprisoned and beheaded,
does anything remain? –
His self less human way of life,
their selfish human shame.

© 2000 Stainer & Bell Ltd

Metre: 7.6.8.6.

Written 17 January 1997

I do not know of any other hymn which follows the story of John the Baptist right through to his death.

5 Christ, we do not recognise

EARLHAM   *Nicholas Williams (1959–)*

Christ, we do not re-cog-nise your face in all the world; nei - ther do we
un-der-stand the love to which we're called.
longs to meet that need.

© 2002 Stainer & Bell Ltd

Christ, we do not recognise
your face in all the world;
neither do we understand
the love to which we're called.

Christ we do not understand
compassion's power and course;
neither do we empathise
with those who need its force.

Christ we do not empathise
when dearth confronts our greed;
neither do we recognise
love longs to meet that need.

© 2000 Stainer & Bell Ltd

Metre: 7.6.7.6. Trochaic

Written 25 January 1997

Geoffrey Duncan has edited a book entitled 'Seeing Christ in Others', something, surely, that all Christians are called upon to do. 'As much as you did it for the least of these ...'

6 Rising sun and leaping fire

RISING SUN   Ian Sharp (1943–)

Ris - ing sun and leap - ing fire,__ shards of ice and fleece of snow; in -

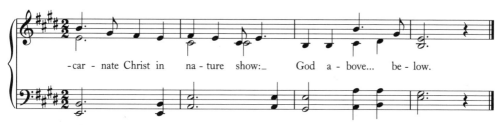

-car - nate Christ in na - ture show:__ God a - bove... be - low.

© 2002 Stainer & Bell Ltd

Rising sun and leaping fire,
shards of ice and fleece of snow;
incarnate Christ in nature show:
God above... below.

Riven tide and hidden rock,
sun and supernova's might,
through fractured faith and fallen night
shines God's given light.

Light extinguished, God-head quelled:
hung alone where nature stood,
a crown of thorns, a cross of wood
raged against the good.

Rising sun and leaping fire:
gentle, loving spirit show,
ascended Christ with nature flow
God above... below.

© 1997 Stainer & Bell Ltd

Metre: 7.7 8 5.

Written 25 January 1997

Inspired by a talk on Celtic spirituality given by Philip Berry, a British Methodist Minister. First published in 'Worship Live' No. 10.

7 Into the gulf, the silent space

REVERE

John R. Kleinheksel Sr (1938–)

In - to the gulf, the si - lent space, where faith is lost for words, where sense and rea - son flee and fall, where com - fort seems ab - surd: speak - -ing to feel - ings deep with - in,_____ God's still small voice dis - turbs.

© 2002 Stainer & Bell Ltd

Heard at the point where thoughts are lost,
where meaning loses force,
where earthquake, wind and fire are stilled,
compassion's quiet resource:
the tender thunder of that love
that counters holocaust.

Still is the mind that hears that voice,
quiet to receive its strain;
open to argument and hope,
finding its faith through pain,
lifting all life through passion's praise,
reaching for heaven's plain.

© 2000 Stainer & Bell Ltd

Metre: 8.6.8.6.8.6.

Written 31 March 1997

Inspired by the words of a clergyman depicted on the BBC television soap 'EastEnders'.

8 Silent like the lamb that's slaughtered

BRUISED REED   *Marlene Phillips (1933–)*

Si - lent like the lamb that's slaugh - tered, still to be your sons and daugh - ters?
Or will e - ven you dis - own us, turn your back, des - pise, de - throne us;
shroud - ing light, con - sum - ing hope, thrust - ing us be - yond love's scope?

Why are we so lost, forsaken?
Kindle, God, some expectation:
mend the reed that's bruised and bending,
fan the smouldering ember, flaming ·
into love we know as real,
into grace, our hurt to heal.

Then, when scars of violation
spurn each act of re-creation,
and the church, itself, abusing,
in derision, trust confusing,
multiplies our powerless plight;
let us not succumb, but fight!

Words © 1997 and Music © 1998 Stainer & Bell Ltd

Metre: 8 8.8 8.7 7.

Written 12 June 1997

Even the church disowns those whom society despises and, far from loving those who might point to scandal, it turns its back on them. The text relates to abuse/harassment and is linked to the allegations of sexual harassment within the Methodist Church. At Conference 1997 there was a call to hold a minute's silence in recognition of those so harassed. The 'silence' of the hymn reflects that silence of those who dare not complain for fear of ridicule or dismissal. First published in 'Worship Live' No. 10.

9   When relativity is lost

When relativity is lost,
when time has flown its course,
when matter has contracted,
when light returns to source;
we find the imprint of your power,
the function of your gaze,
the lightness of compassion,
the love that will amaze.

Within this endless round of things,
of seasons, nights and days
that language calls creation,
this riddled, teasing maze,
we must learn how to see again,
to open up our eyes
to sense the world like children,
God's place to realise.

© 2000 Stainer & Bell Ltd

Metre: 8.6.7.6.D.

Written 4 May 1997

Is it possible for us, through child-like eyes, to see what lies behind creation?

ATTLEBOROUGH

Peter Cutts (1937–)

When re-la-ti-vi-ty is lost, when time has flown its course, when mat-ter has con-trac-ted, when light re-turns to source; we find the im-print of your power, the func-tion of your gaze, the light-ness of com-pass-ion, the love that will a-maze.

© 2002 Stainer & Bell Ltd for the world except USA and Canada

10   How could our language frame the form?

How could our language frame the form
that gave our comprehension birth,
the native ground of all we are,
that bore the stars, that made the earth?

Can wonder sense the bounds of love,
or understand the deep despair,
that brought a nameless God to search
for progeny that love to share?

When all the wonder of each age
is pooled with those as yet unborn,
astounded still, we'll stagger stunned,
by all that we have left to learn.

We'll walk through glades of mystery,
and at each bough we'll stand and stare
at hidden sights, as yet unseen,
of all that God has brought to bear.

© 2000 Stainer & Bell Ltd

Metre: LM

Suggested Tunes: ROCKINGHAM and GIFT OF LOVE

Written 18 June 1997

*Written after reading 'The Handmaid of Piety' by Edward Houghton – a book about the hymns of
Charles Wesley. 'Rockingham' is often associated with 'When I survey the wondrous cross' by Isaac
Watts. Watts saw a close interrelation between nature and salvation, an allusion which goes well with
these words.*

See time's brief history ending
in God, as it began;
the stellar consummation
of rhythm, scheme and plan.
The brush of wave on shingle,
the hush of turning tide,
are part of the procession,
the cosmic coaster ride.

The city, once imagined,
a scene so hard to grasp:
artistic ultimatum,
built on a scale so vast,
is no more than a vision
and no less than a dream;
beyond our calm conception,
above our wildest scheme.

Life's language will but falter,
its grammar never last;
each argument and reason
fade quickly in the past;
for love is more than language,
and God is more than grace:
beyond articulation,
the goal of time and space.

© 2000 Stainer & Bell Ltd

Metre: 7.6.7.6.D.

Suggested Tunes: KING'S LYNN and AURELIA

Written 22 June 1997

The opening line finds its origin in the title of the book by Stephen Hawking, 'A Brief History of Time'. Originally I had written: 'Time's brief history culminates/In God, as it began;' The metre of these lines did not then match that of the opening lines of later verses and hence the revision. Line 3 of verse 3 read 'The rhythm and the scansion'. My wife suggested that 'scansion' was an obscure word, hence that revision.

12   Scandalous love – I dare not name

Scandalous love – I dare not name –
the love God has for me;
no other love could penetrate
these walls to set me free.

Consummate calm will soothe away
all fretting, care and stress,
when to this table I return,
where God will reach to bless.

Diffident praise, my sole response:
I warrant no reward.
I wonder at the love God shows,
my gratitude record.

© 2000 Stainer & Bell Ltd

Metre: CM

Suggested Tune: MARTYRDOM

Written July 1997

Written at the Hymn Society Conference in York during a session led by Carl Daw Jr. God's love is scandalous because it cuts across conventional judgements to demonstrate the value of discarded people. The tune reminds us that those who embrace the 'scandalous love' of God do not always have an easy time!

13   So death strides on and claims another victim

So death strides on and claims another victim,
another life is ground into the dust;
and all our words are worthless, void and empty,
another coarse betrayal of your trust.

How can we go on passively believing,
how can we stand and watch and not protest?
You've given life, can there be no evasion
of agony and strife, no path to rest?

O God, what is the game that you are playing?
Are we just pieces on some chequered board?
Are you forever deaf to our lamenting,
indifferent to the stress that you accord?

Forgive this doubt, but you have given reason
for us to falter in the path of faith;
we read that you will never fail or alter,
but life feels cold and lonely in this place.

If you have heard, O God, will you not answer
our cries that echo from the dawn of time.
O God, amid this pain and manic laughter,
help us to grasp again our riddled rhyme.

© 2000 Stainer & Bell Ltd

Metre: 11.10.11.10. Iambic

Suggested Tune: INTERCESSOR

Written 10 August 1997

For the late Elizabeth Bolton, in memory of her sister Doris, who was killed in a road accident.

How far are we from all it means
to bear the name of Jesus Christ;
how far from healing ruptured seams
that tear our faith and fault our life?

We utter words that voice intent
to share each heritage and gift,
but actions nullify debate
exaggerating every rift.

We praise an undivided God,
yet set up dams to stem the grace
which pours, a eucharistic flood,
into each fractured interface.

Our God is one; may we be one
in spite of every pain and cost,
as we let go our treasure trove
to grasp the love of Pentecost.

© 2000 Stainer & Bell Ltd

Metre: LM

Suggested Tunes: BRESLAU and CONDITOR ALME

Written 13 September 1997

Written at the Bolton and Rochdale District Synod of the Methodist Church, in response to words of Sister Maureen Farrell, Manchester Ecumenical Officer at the time.

Where is God? For God seems absent
from our praise and from our prayer;
at the limits of our seeing,
will we find the Godhead there?

Where is God? When we are sharing
in this eucharistic feast,
in this faultless celebration,
will we find that promised peace?

Where is God? In saint or saviour?
In the hated and abused
here is God, beside, among us;
God, still silent, still accused.

© 2000 Stainer & Bell Ltd

Metre: 8.7.8.7. Trochaic

Suggested Tunes: ST OSWALD and FOR THE BREAD

Written 20 September 1997

This text was inspired by my reading of 'I cannot find Thee! Still on restless pinion' by Eliza Scudder, and 'Go not my soul, in search of Him' by F. L. Hosmer, both of which were included in the Primitive Methodist Hymnal Supplement. Sometimes we are so absorbed in 'doing it right' that we may lose sight of God.

We cannot judge how well you met the pattern
of Christ, who died to seal God's love for you;
we only sense that you are well rewarded:
a faithful servant, grace has seen you through;
    and so we come, O God, in grief and sorrow;
    Lord, let your comfort fall like morning dew.
    Through your compassion bring a bright tomorrow,
    where tears are dried and love is making all things new.

A singing soul, you brought such joy and pleasure
into our lives, a source of light and hope;
you shared our joy, brought comfort in disaster,
cut through our fears and showed us how to cope;
    and when, O God, we rustle with that laughter,
    the rhyme of love keeps happiness alive;
    help us to treasure now and ever after
    each gift and grace for which we seek to live and strive.

And so we give you back to God who gave you
to share our lives awhile upon this earth.
as yet we wait in faith to share your triumph,
of life renewed, new life, through heaven's birth:
    a life beyond all hope and comprehension,
    a joy transcending fear and human wrong,
    a love that holds us safe beyond the tension
    of worldly strife where we will join in heaven's song.

© 2000 Stainer & Bell Ltd

Metre: 11.10.11.10.11.10.11.12.

Suggested Tune: LONDONDERRY AIR

Written 7 November 1997

These words were written as a reflection on the emotions I felt while watching a video of the funeral of Diana, Princess of Wales. The first halves of the first and second verses are intentionally addressed to the deceased, the second halves to God in respect of that person. The final verse breaks the pattern to acknowledge the action in which we are participating and the hope on which it is founded.

You move with unexpected pace,
you whirl our lives around;
your actions seem devoid of grace,
your suddenness astounds.

You tear the lives we love and know,
each joyful dream you break;
our expectations cease to grow,
our hopes no longer wake.

You harrow ground that we have tilled,
you echo every act;
your shadow overcasts the field,
you shatter every fact.

It seems we cannot live secure,
each prop and hope is gone,
the way ahead no longer sure
beneath this dying Son.

How can we trust if you are deaf
to every plea and prayer;
if you can grant just one request
God, show us you are there!

© 2000 Stainer & Bell Ltd

Metre: CM

Suggested Tunes: THIS ENDRIS NYGHT and DETROIT

Written 17 November 1997

Dedicated to Elizabeth Bolton, this is a hymn of lament following the sudden death of a loved one.

Life proclaims God's glory,
fuelling our desire;
manifests the story
hid in wind and fire.

Colour, made untarnished,
moistened by the rain,
burnished by the sunlight,
fills creation's frame.

God of awe and wonder
speaks through such as these:
rainbow, stars or thunder
bring us to our knees.

© 2000 Stainer & Bell Ltd

Metre: 6.5.6.5. Trochaic

Suggested Tunes: GLENFINLAS and BEMERTON (FILITZ)

Written 10 November 1997

Written after reading the poem 'A Storm', by Keith Douglas. The text touches on my own experience of conversion as a result of awe at the wonder of creation.

We thank you God for those who know
your depth of wisdom in their lives,
whose pride or power do not prevent
the love of Christ from being shown.

We thank you for the scholar's skill,
the learning that is honed and trained,
the gifts, that given, now are used
for good, for care, for love, for all.

We thank you for the singing soul
that soars to some harmonious height
above, beyond our human sense,
and glimpses heaven, almost whole.

We thank you for the poet's art
that offers prophecy and light,
which through the rhythm of the words
remains with us when thoughts depart.

We thank you for incisive sight
that analyses and discerns,
through science, patterns that inform
predictions, actions we repeat.

We thank you for the dancing form
that pirouettes with grace and skill,
that weaves a pattern through the air
and challenges our static norm.

We thank you, God, for light and sound
with which we interact and move:
for singing colours, thrumming beat,
that thrill, that shake the solid ground.

We thank you, God, for all the gifts
of human spirit, skill and mind;
O may indifference never numb
our sense of awe at love so deft.

© 2000 Stainer & Bell Ltd

Metre: LM

Suggested Tune: WAREHAM

Written 19 November 1997

I have two nieces, Hannah and Emma Daniels. Hannah sings and teaches. Emma is a philosopher and teacher. My son Jonathan was an interactive artist. This hymn is for them, and for anyone else whose skills are included! The pattern is intentionally experimental with the first and last lines of each verse rhyming, and then not always completely. Pick and mix!

The sunlight on the water
sets singing in our eyes
a single glance of wonder,
a shimmering first surprise;
but dusty practicalities,
the thorn within our flesh,
that recommend obedience
just will not let us rest.

The landfall at a haven,
our solitude replete,
a foretaste of God's heaven,
serenity complete,
is tempered by reality
with feet firm on the ground.
We recognise a call to live
in this world's sight and sound.

We turn again from wonder,
from spiritual surprise,
from laser light and thunder,
through dazzled, dancing eyes
we see the grinding poverty,
we smell the stench of death,
and only sacrificial love
will lead through hell to rest.

© 2000 Stainer & Bell Ltd

Metre: 7.6.7.6.8.6.8.6.

Written 22 November 1997

I wrote the first verse after reading the opening pages of Melvyn Bragg's 'Credo'. The last line of the last verse alludes to the Apostles' Creed: 'He descended into hell, on the third day he rose again from the dead .' Whenever we are attracted to our being lifted out of the world by our spiritual experience, God has a habit of putting us right back in it again — as Elijah, the disciples on the Mount of Transfiguration, and St Paul knew so well.

CHRYSOSTOM

Peter Cutts (1937–)

The sun-light on the wa – ter sets sing-ing in our eyes a
sin-gle glance of won – der, a shimmer-ing first sur – prise; but
dus – ty prac-ti – – ca-li – ties, the thorn with-in our flesh, that
re – com – mend o – be – di – ence just will not let us rest.

© 2002 Stainer & Bell Ltd for the world except USA and Canada

God forgive our tabloid praise,
glossing over grief and loss:
empty praise of empty words,
treating life as so much dross.

Love is real but so is grief.
Jesus wept and so can we;
all our swaying, chanting songs
can't remove life's agony.

Don't we care? Or is this right?
Have we just not understood?
Did Christ die immune from pain
hanging on that cross of wood?

Yet we sing our casual songs
shielded from this cosmic drought;
hail expediency as God,
pleasure all we seek, or sought.

But if he received that prize,
how can we expect for more?
Help us, God, to find a way
back through life to praise that's pure.

© 2000 Stainer & Bell Ltd

Metre: 7.7.7.7.

Suggested Tune: MONKLAND

Written 20 November 1997

This text was written as a reflection on the sometimes shallow nature of certain styles of modern hymns and songs. The brightness of this tune adds, I think, a certain irony.

O God, beyond all thought
a finite mind can grasp,
we offer you the dawning day,
each present need or task.

O God, beyond constraint
of matter, time or space,
there is no vacuum, void or ground
unfurnished by your grace.

O God, beyond all sight,
of light and love the source,
we trust ourselves in life or death
to your eternal course.

© 2000 Stainer & Bell Ltd

Metre: SM

Suggested Tune: ST MICHAEL

Written 23 November 1997

An exploration of the omnipresence of God.

The kindling sun will light my way
as power bursts through the world.
O light of hope, illumine day,
as love is fresh, unfurled.

The ebb and flow of every tide
transforms the life I live;
a parable on every side
of all God has to give.

Then here my seeds of faith I'll sow,
creation's nest and fold;
secure in God, yes, here I'll grow
till heaven's taken hold.

© 2000 Stainer & Bell Ltd

Metre: CM

Suggested Tunes: ARDEN and AZMON

Written 23 November 1997

Another hymn inspired by a fruitful talk on Celtic spirituality given by Philip Berry, a British Methodist Minister (see page 7).

24   Who would risk such desolation?

LITTLEHAM CROSS

Peter Cutts (1937–)

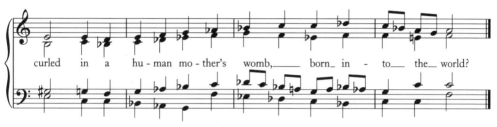

© 2002 Stainer & Bell Ltd for the world except USA and Canada

Who would risk such desolation,
no more safely curled
in a human mother's womb,
born into the world?

Who would furnish liberation,
all God's care to prove,
seeking out the poor, bereft,
with incarnate love?

Who would welcome crucifixion
with her arms outstretched,
watching hers and God's own son
source of holiness.

God, the ground of all creation
enters every pain,
lives each fear and dies each death
yet to rise again.

© 2000 Stainer & Bell Ltd

Metre: 8.5.7.5.

Written 23 November 1997

An exploration of the incarnation. The verses range through God, Christ, Mary and back to God. I am fascinated by the Catholic emphasis on the importance of the role of Mary who, while not taking the place of Jesus and not being divine, is essentially very special.

From sunrise on a cloudless day
God's light has grown with every hour;
eternal light that never dies,
that fills the earth with life and power.

When Israel sought a desert path
a cloud was visible by day,
but through the night, from dusk to dawn,
a fiery pillar lit their way.

God turned their darkness into light:
resplendent sun of righteousness,
eternal glory, never spent,
with warmth to nurture, shone to bless.

And so the light of God will last
through every span and phase of time,
to guide us through our wilderness,
the light of Christ will always shine.

© 1997, 2000 Stainer & Bell Ltd

Metre: LM

Suggested Tunes: WARRINGTON and DUNEDIN

Written 25 November 1997

Written for the dedication of new lighting at Wigan Road Methodist Church, Leigh, Lancashire on 30 November 1997, with the following first verse:

The work we dedicate today:
The lamps we see, wires hid from sight,
Are witness to creative gifts
And God's command, 'Let there be light'.

and this penultimate verse:

Now sharing God's creative task,
We work with skill to train each ray;
We sing with joy, 'Let there be light',
Lord, let our darkness shine like day.

I was determined to include the name of one of the main people involved in this project – 'Ray' (Davenport)!

26   See the glory: pavements glisten

See the glory: pavements glisten,
carollers are now in sight;
see the silver star, that's risen,
shining through the frosty night.

Watch the shoppers stand at windows:
moving figures beckon, glow;
shining crib and cartoon shadows:
see excitement spread and grow.

Witness child-like adult wonder
at each winning sound or sight;
hear the laughter, soft as thunder,
ringing through this chilling night.

Glimpsed, you're huddled, cramped and sodden
in the doorway's frozen chill;
do you wonder you're forgotten,
Jesus, waiting for us still?

© 1997, 2000 Stainer & Bell Ltd

Metre: 8.7.8.7. Trochaic

Suggested Tunes: OTTERY ST MARY and EMMAUS

Written 27 November 1997

Inspired by the 1997 Christmas lights in Northwich, Cheshire. 'Pavements' can equally be 'sidewalks'. The third verse was added during September 2000. Originally the first line read 'See the glory, more than glimmer'. Published in the 'Methodist Recorder'. Tunes of a sombre nature have been chosen, thus setting off the last verse.

Stories unfold, a mathematical tune
guiding the words like the weft on a loom;
intricate spirals and webs of delight,
shining with dew as the dawn ends the night.
The pattern, the purpose, we seek to appraise
is no confirmation of God, or God's ways.

Words left unguarded, or chained to a thought,
canonised, catechised, dogmatised, taught;
wrought into creeds and passed down age to age;
Testament, scripture, so we name the page.
It says in the Bible that we should believe
but this is no proof we should blindly receive.

We'll not reach up to take hold of the hope,
nor can our children yet ration God's scope.
Faith that we fathom, the love that holds fast,
prizes like these are beyond human grasp;
for, just when we think that we've made God our own,
the spirit wind changes, the caged bird has flown.

© 2000 Stainer & Bell Ltd

Metre: 10 10.10 10.11 11.

Written 2 December 1997

On 'Start the Week', a BBC radio programme, a mathematician was talking about the patterns that repeat unexpectedly throughout the cosmos. The observation and understanding of such patterns does not provide incontrovertible proof of a creator. Neither does the Bible; 'because the Bible tells me so' is not a satisfactory ground for belief. We are left with faith, which is no more and no less than a gift of God's grace. Let us just be thankful when that gift is ours. Our descriptions of God are bounded by metaphor. Just when we think we've got God tied down, experience changes our perception.

SHENSTONE

Peter Cutts (1937–)

Sto-ries un-fold, a mathe-ma-ti-cal tune guid-ing the words like the
weft on a loom; in-tri-cate spi-rals and webs of de-light,
shin-ing with dew as the dawn ends the night. The pat-tern, the pur-pose, we
seek to ap-praise is no con-fir-ma-tion of God, or God's ways.

© 2002 Stainer & Bell Ltd for the world except USA and Canada

HOLY INNOCENTS   Ian Sharp (1943–)

He - rod's high and migh - ty stand   showed the power at his com - mand,

slaugh - tered chil - dren in the   land:___ Ky - ri - e, Lord have mer - cy,

descant for V.6

Ky - ri - e, Lord have mer - cy, Ky - ri - e, Lord have mer - cy on us.

* Optional: the Chorus may be sung by a separate group

© 2002 Stainer & Bell Ltd

Herod's high and mighty stand
showed the power at his command,
slaughtered children in the land:
> *Kyrie, Lord have mercy,*
> *Kyrie, Lord have mercy,*
> *Kyrie, Lord have mercy on us.*

Mary wept, she understood,
wept as every mother should,
Ramah's echo, death to good:
Chorus

Surely force has had its day,
brutish whim and power's display;
yet our actions hurt, betray:
Chorus

Seen on every paper's page,
words of hate and fists of rage,
signs of greed in every age:
Chorus

Anger still inflicts the pain,
each excuse is seen as lame,
yet again we bear the shame:
Chorus

Till through this and every time
people cease from heinous crime,
till with peace their actions rhyme:
Chorus

© 1999 Stainer & Bell Ltd

Metre: 7 7 7. and Chorus 7 7.9.

Written 28 December 1997

Written on Holy Innocents Day for that day. The chorus was added when the text was included in 'Songs for the New Millennium', where it appeared after verses 2, 4 and 6.

THE CRADLE   *Marlene Phillips (1933–)*

I ached to hold the child I bore,
but when I held you, you were still;
a life had come and gone again,
your brow was cold and chill.

You limply lay within my arms;
I looked into your closing eyes,
and all the words of comfort came
and seemed like empty lies.

'God gives and God will take away';
but you had scarcely breathed a breath.
What was the point? What scheme or plan
required your infant death?

O child of faulted, faded dreams,
while disembodied hopes cascade,
you leave unanswered questions strewn,
but love will never fade.

Words © 2000 and Music © 2002 Stainer & Bell Ltd

Metre: 8.8.8.6.

Written 18 January 1998

The text tries to make sense of stillbirth and infant death. When the Chancellor of the Exchequer Gordon Brown and his wife, Sarah, lost their child, Jennifer, I sent this hymn to them. They responded appreciatively and it is dedicated to them. It had originally been written after listening to a mother talking on the BBC programme 'Songs of Praise', and concluded with the following in place of verse 4:

And in it all, amidst the tears,
the guilt, the anguish and the shame,
as years have passed, your love has stayed,
as yesterday, the same.

O child of expectation's hope,
an expectation shattered, scorned;
you left unanswered questions strewn,
yet love was not still-born.

30 We gaze in wonder at the morning's dawning

GAZE IN WONDER

Anne Jarrett (1954–)

We gaze in won-der at the morn-ing's dawn-ing, pos-it-ive wit-ness to God's faith-ful grace; we turn our backs, and in the sha-dow stand-ing, shield the light we need to find our place.

In arrogance, in darkness we will stumble,
screening our eyes, we turn away from light.
We venerate our skill, the rocket's rumble,
deadens sense, distorting wrong and right.

As stewards of love, let's contemplate creation,
filigree frosting of a winter's pain;
God holds in hand elation, desperation,
born in death that we might live again.

Words © 2000 and Music © 2002 Stainer & Bell Ltd

Metre: 11.10.11.9.

Written 23 January 1998

Too often, from self-sufficient pride, we turn our back on the help we need.

When myth and magic lose their sway
and sentiment has died;
when all the props are swept away
on which we once relied;
within that vacuum we can find
a faith that's tested, tried.

When life and death are merged in one
and meaning loses force;
when those we love have gone away
and, shattered by remorse,
we turn towards infinity,
we face compassion's source.

Then, at the closing of our day,
when life has run to ground,
we face the proof of who we are,
of all we've done or found;
may we, with angels and with friends,
the cause of praise resound.

© 2000 Stainer & Bell Ltd

Metre: 8.6.8.6.8.6.

Suggested Tune: REVERE (John R. Kleinheksel Sr) *(see page 8)*

Written 7 January 1998

Sometimes it is only when we have apparently lost faith that we really find what matters most.

We cannot be Christian until we are free;
our systems and structures just won't let us be
good news to the people, the poor, the oppressed,
the prisoner, the homeless, whom Christ sought to bless.

Disdainful we watch politicians collide,
so safe in self-interest, inflated with pride,
as, treasuring status, encouraging greed,
they prostitute language, and denigrate need.

And yet, in our comfort, complacent we sit,
refusing the pearl just because of the grit;
hypocrisy reigns, as we muddle and laugh,
the risk of God's change is too scary by half;

For we are no better than those we deride:
encompassed in falsehood and cushioned by pride;
our thundering indifference, our deafening deceit,
denies all the praise that we heap at God's feet.

© 2001 Stainer & Bell Ltd

Metre: 11 11.11 11.

Suggested Tunes: DATCHET and FOUNDATION

Written 7 February 1998

Christians speak of being free, but often we are constrained by a misinterpretation of Christianity or by convention.

Watchmen wait in expectation,
wait the coming of the dawn;
keep the charge that they've been given,
faithful to the vow they've sworn.
> Now, amidst anticipation,
> keep us faithful to your task,
> till you greet us, loving Saviour,
> this is all we seek or ask.

Bridesmaids wait in expectation,
each lamp trimmed with hopeful flame;
wait the bridegroom, at his coming
he will call them each by name.
> Now, amidst anticipation,
> keep us faithful to your task,
> till you greet us, loving Saviour,
> this is all we seek or ask.

Still we wait in expectation,
wait the coming of your word;
keep alight the faith we carry,
that our hope may be assured.
> Now, amidst anticipation,
> keep us faithful to your task,
> till you greet us, loving Saviour,
> till we're welcomed home at last.

© 2000 Stainer & Bell Ltd

Metre: 8.7.8.7.D.

Written 10 February 1998

Suggested Tunes: THERE'S A LIGHT UPON THE MOUNTAINS and AUTHORITY

Watchmen and bridesmaids anticipate the rule of God in the Old and New Testaments respectively. Note the contrast with a modern wedding. Biblically, the bridesmaids await the bridegroom! The tune 'There's a light upon the mountains' was originally set to Henry Burton's Advent text and thus matches the mood of these words very well.

As riddles ramify Ezekiel's prose,
they make his mystic manner more than pose;
then wheels and whirring spirits fill his head,
make signs and wonders pointing where God led.

So honey tasting were the scrolls he took,
that visions filled the skies, the mountains shook;
then magic coloured silence in his mind
just hinting at the paradox he'd find.

Though still in exile, he was not bereft,
his vivid fears were faded by God's breath.
Look: bones devoid of flesh first fill the scene,
and now they're dancing where decay had been.

Then, see, a temple skilfully re-built
arises from the rubble and the silt.
And from it flows a river; either side
the verdant vegetation spreads and thrives.

And all that once was barren, dead or void,
our God with love has finally destroyed;
those visions that seemed hair-brained, cracked or worse
now offer hope, no longer seem perverse.

© 2000 Stainer & Bell Ltd

Metre: 10 10.10 10.

Suggested Tunes: CHILTON FOLIAT and SHELDONIAN

Written 11 February 1998

There are few hymns which address this vision of Ezekiel apart from the African-American Spiritual 'Dry Bones'.

To feel the heat, the rush of air,
the shattered caution, searing flare;
the glittering fragments, shards of glass,
the sudden, sickly, thunderous blast;

Then through the haze, the settling dust,
the crumpled bodies, mangled trust;
in eerie silence, standing still
I scream in anger at 'God's will'.

Yet God would never sanction pain,
or shatter lives for greater gain;
confound such sentimental dross.
But where is God amidst this loss?

© 2000 Stainer & Bell Ltd

Metre: LM

Suggested Tunes: WILDERNESS and ERHALT' UNS, HERR

Written 5 March 1998

The Arndale Centre in Manchester had been bombed. This text is a reflection on that terrorism, written a year later. This seems even more pertinent since 11 September 2001. I feel that the tunes, particularly 'Wilderness', are well matched to the words.

To a world so torn and tortured
came the voice of one who knew
what it cost to lift oppression,
challenge the accepted view.

John convicted crowds before him,
charged hypocrisy with God;
opened up the way for Jesus
who would follow where he trod.

Then, imprisoned, John was silenced;
yet a voice more powerful still
challenged in and out of season
all who heard to do God's will.

Living, Christ would lift oppression,
dying, he would seem to fail,
crying out in desolation,
yet God's love would still prevail.

© 2000 Stainer & Bell Ltd

Metre: 8.7.8.7. Trochaic

Suggested Tunes: WRAYSBURY and CHARLESTOWN

Written 8 March 1998

A text that explores John the Baptist's role as the forerunner of Christ.

Why do you bother, gracious friend,
with one whose love is cold?
Your eyes have caught my gaze again,
they charm, convict and hold.

Was this the glance that Peter glimpsed
across a courtyard's space,
that stopped him in his tracks in tears
and caused his heart to race?

Was this the warmth that, from the cross,
held John and Mary's gaze,
as turning to each other's arms
they found in pain God's praise?

O love that sought them, find a way
to fuse my heart of stone;
O gracious friend, O loving fire,
come, make my heart your home.

© 2002 Stainer & Bell Ltd

Metre: CM

Suggested Tune: GERONTIUS

Written 21 April 1998

If we were to look into the face of Jesus, would we not wonder 'Why do you bother, gracious friend?'

What if the Babel consequence
of language, race or creed could fall,
and open paths to peacefulness
dividing none, uniting all?

The internet infused with love
might give a means to gain that goal:
a web of true relationships
with fear removed, and then made whole.

In seconds we can link with those
across the street, around the globe;
could this, then, be a means to weave
all people in a seamless robe?

If this is so a vision dawns:
our science, yet, may offer hope
to fold God's world-wide family
within a love of boundless scope.

So let us use each new found skill
as once a Saviour crafted wood,
and through our faith's integrity
use all God's gifts for human good.

© 2000 Stainer & Bell Ltd

Metre: LM

Suggested Tunes: HERONGATE and WAREHAM

Written 17 May 1998

A text arising from an unusual invitation from the musician David Lee: to write a hymn in celebration of the Revd Stoker Wilson's appointment to a post to promote electronic communication within the Diocese of Durham.

June Baker (1936–)

© 1999 Stainer & Bell Ltd

Great God of many names:
Jehovah,[1] Allah,[2] Lord,
Christ, Brahman,[3] Spirit, Adonai;[4]
we worship you.
Whatever name,
whichever face,
we worship you.

With pomp and pageantry
beneath an onion dome,[5]
or in a bare and simple room,[6]
we worship you.
Chorus

With tabla[11] or guitar,
or with a thousand lights,[12]
through fasting, feasting, fellowship
we worship you.
Chorus

In chapel, mosque[7] or shrine[8]
we wait to praise your name,
through icon,[9] sitar,[10] book or choir
we worship you.
Chorus

With formal dress or free,
we meditate or dance,
through pesach,[13] hajj[14] or nam simran[15]
we worship you.
Chorus

Whatever name or creed,
enlightenment or book,
we seek you through our pilgrimage
and worship you.

© 1999 Stainer & Bell Ltd

Metre: 6.6.8.4. and Chorus 4.4.4.

Written May 1998

Without our denying the differences separating faiths, we have a desperate need to recognise the common features that bind the major world religions together. Even Hinduism, traditionally viewed as a polytheistic religion, has a monotheistic basis, if properly understood, but with many manifestations of the Godhead. A Muslim child said: 'My God has many names'. We must talk together, work together and learn how to worship together. It is my hope and expectation that during this century the relationship between religions will go through the same pilgrimage towards understanding, co-operation and mutual recognition as Christian denominations have done through the ecumenical movement of the twentieth century.

'Great God of Many Names', first published in 'Sound Bytes' with a beautifully evocative tune written by June Baker, is offered to this end.

[1] Hebrew: transliteration of YHWH
[2] Muslim name for God
[3] Hindu name for God
[4] Hebrew = Lord
[5] Allusion to Orthodox Christianity
[6] Allusion to Christian Puritanism or the Society of Friends
[7] Islamic place of worship
[8] Buddhist (and other faith's) place of meditation/worship
[9] Allusion to Orthodox Christianity
[10] Traditional Indian musical instrument
[11] Traditional Indian musical instrument
[12] Hindu festival of Divali
[13] Passover (Judaism)
[14] Pilgrimage (Islam)
[15] Repetition of the divine name (Sikhism)

Outrageous love that dares to breach
the dam of our desire,
the crumbling edifice of fear
that harbours hidden fire;

Contentious care, that cuts across
our prejudice and cant,
revealing hidden depths of love
where we refuse to plant;

Unbidden grace that petrifies
the action we would take,
that renders mute our words of hate,
while heaven's comfort breaks;

Enigma: friend, Messiah, God;
while hypocrites despair
you die to love discarded souls;
enable our repair.

© 2000 Stainer & Bell Ltd

Metre: CM

Suggested Tune: ST PETER

Written 31 May 1998

A reflection on the enigmatic, scandalous love of God demonstrated by Jesus's concern for the outcast.

Angels watch in awestruck wonder:
cradled in a mother's arms,
source of silence, whispered thunder,
gurgling, giggling, now disarms.

God, whose breath inspired creation:
suckled at a mother's breast.
God of peace and consternation
wriggling, never seems to rest.

Restless parent, God, all seeing:
caught in space, cocooned in time;
metamorphosis of being,
mighty power, now humankind.

© 2000 Stainer & Bell Ltd

Metre: 8.7.8.7. Trochaic

Suggested Tunes: GOTT WILL'S MACHEN and STUTTGART

Written 5 August 1998

The babe of Bethlehem is believed by Christians to be the God who created stillness and thunder by breathing through chaos, the God who spoke in a still, small voice to Elijah, the God in whose image humanity is made, the divine parent of us all. This God was 'caught in space, cocooned in time' as Jesus until the chrysalis of life burst open to reveal eternity.

Moved beyond imagination:
see the beauty, gold on gold;
feel the rhythm of the music,
art and artistry unfold.

Now they stand: anticipation,
what will love and life reveal?
End of waiting, new beginning,
words their deepest feelings seal.

Let us join their celebration:
pray for all they wish to share;
love, and loving ever after,
understanding, strength to care;

Then beyond the jubilation,
mutual joy, eternal peace;
that this day may be the tasting,
but their life the lasting feast.

©1999 Stainer & Bell Ltd

Metre: 8.7.8.7. Trochaic

Suggested Tunes: LAUS DEO (REDHEAD 46) and GALILEE

Written 10 August 1998

Written for the marriage of my niece Emma Daniels with Jamie Burstow. The sight of Emma at the fitting of her gold-coloured wedding dress inspired the first two lines, and the hymn was sung at their wedding on 13 February 1999 in Comberbach Methodist Church.

As our congregation gathers
lift our lives, with love amaze;
offer some melodious treasure,
fill our hearts with wondering praise.
Crashing brass and singing cymbals,
soaring organ, sound and light;
fill this space with awe and thunder,
lift us through the veil of night.

Then a sudden, silent stillness
holds an echo in the air:
on a knife edge, balanced, waiting,
in the silence, you are there.
Joy beyond imagination,
love incarnate, hope to hold,
faith we cannot sound or fathom,
gripped in wonder, we behold.

© 2000 Stainer & Bell Ltd

Metre: 8.7.8.7.D.

Suggested Tunes: CALON LAN and CHARLESTOWN. (When CHARLESTOWN is used each stanza is broken into two verses.)

Written 31 August 1998

A hymn of invocation. Anticipation at the beginning of worship can depend on sound and silence, environment and music. As the opening music dies away an echo hangs, as it were, in the air. In that transient stillness I sense a heightened awareness of the presence of God. Now we are ready!

Such enchantment, sudden strangeness,
power and love, by God, distilled;
then they recognise his presence,
by his words their fears are stilled.
    'Peace be with you', Simon Peter,
    John, you need not be afraid;
    'Peace be with you', doubting Thomas,
    don't be anxious or dismayed.

In the garden he saw Mary,
talked with her, unrecognised;
naming her drew back the curtain,
opened tear-stained, blinded eyes.
    Others walking to Emmaus
    talked, depressed; their sadness showed,
    till at last, their journey ended,
    broken bread their Lord disclosed.

Fishing, from a boat, some saw him,
they had trawled, had felt forlorn;
recognition added savour
to their breakfast at the dawn.
    As we go about our business
    bring enchantment to our lives;
    open eyes that we might know the
    love from which our peace derives.

© 2000 Stainer & Bell Ltd

Metre: 8.7.8.7.D.

Suggested Tune: HYFRYDOL

Written 2 October 1998

Inspired by the song 'Some enchanted evening' and written for Tyldesley Methodist Church.

Enslaved by debt, a world-wide grief
cries out through pain for liberty;
the chains that bound us in the past
ensure today's captivity.

Our greed for wealth, our selfishness,
will hold us in indifference,
and others starve and die because
we will not share God's providence.

Enslaved by fear, we need to risk
the loss that others ought to gain
that, from self-sacrificial love,
new joy may grow from seeds of pain.

Then from this season's hopelessness
help us to set each other free;
and when our only debt is love,
Lord, share our joy at Jubilee.

© 2000 Stainer & Bell Ltd

Metre: LM

Suggested Tune: BRESLAU

Written 5 October 1998

Written as we moved towards the millennium, this hymn reflects on world debt and the need for Jubilee.

The shore of God that breaks our prayer:
our simper deadened by the thundering shingle,
the crash of pleading, and the broken promise;
our love, but never God's receding.

The pools that mirror human hope
disturbed and fractured by our own transgression;
the faith, once limpet like, dislodged and drifting,
stuttering statements tossed by life's collision.

The ebb and flow of countless days,
the tide's regression, dreams left dry and stranded;
and this is all we glimpse in life's procession
until in heaven at last we've landed.

© 2002 Stainer & Bell Ltd

Metre: 8.11.11.9.

Written 27 October 1998

This text offers an exploration of prayer and life using the sea as metaphor. I was brought up in Paignton, within a couple of hundred yards of the south Devon shore.

BUTTERTUBS

Peter Cutts (1937–)

The shore of God_____ that breaks our prayer: our sim - per

dead - ened by the thunder - ing shin - gle,_____ the crash of

plead - ing, and the bro - ken pro - mise; our love, but

nev - er God's re - ced - - ing.

© 2002 Stainer & Bell Ltd for the world except USA and Canada

Long ago God spoke to people,
told them what they ought to do,
showed his love in word and action,
gave them strength and courage too.
Abraham was called to follow,
leave the place where he'd been born:
take his family, leaving early,
putting faith in God at dawn.

Moses couldn't speak too clearly,
but with Aaron at his side,
God made him a mighty leader,
now he had no need to hide.
In the land to which he brought them
people settled, made a home,
but like sheep they wandered freely
from the faith in which they'd grown.

Joshua had helped them conquer,
Saul and David came to rule;
they were never perfect people,
still were learning in God's school.
Prophets came to share God's message,
showed the people right from wrong,
teaching them what they'd forgotten,
giving them a fresh new song.

So Isaiah and Ezekiel,
Jeremiah, Micah too,
joined Hosea, Amos, Jonah,
showing people what to do.
These and many, many others
taught of God's great care and scope;
helped the people live together
offered faith and love and hope.

© 1999 Stainer & Bell Ltd

Metre: 8.7.8.7.D.

Written 30 October 1998

Written for 'Sound Bytes' as a text to celebrate and teach Old Testament history.

David Lee (1956–)

Long a-go God spoke to peo - ple, told them what they ought to do, showed his love in word and ac - tion, gave them strength and cou - rage too. Ab - ra - ham was called to fol - low, leave the place where he'd been born: take his fam - ily, leav - ing ear - ly, put - ting faith in God at dawn.

© 1999 Stainer & Bell Ltd

In the beginning God played with the planets,
set them a-spinning in time and in space,
stars in the night sky, while sun lit the daytime,
blue was the globe that was formed for our race.

God saw the seas and the fish that swam in them,
formed the dry land where the trees soon would grow,
animals now could inhabit the countries
warmed by the oceans or covered in snow.

After the animals, people were coming
made in God's likeness to live on the earth;
big the blue planet God gave them to live on
sharing its riches, its wonder and worth.

© 1999 Stainer & Bell Ltd

Metre: 11.10.11.10. Dactylic

This text may also be sung to STEWARDSHIP

Written 11 November 1998

A text for all-age worship, which takes as its theme the creation story from Genesis 1.

David Lee (1956–)

Triplet swing style (♩♩ = ♩ ♪)

In the be - gin - ning God played____ with the pla - nets,____ set them a - spin - ning in time____ and in space,____ stars in the night sky, while sun lit the day - time,____ blue was the globe that was formed____ for our race.____

© 1999 Stainer & Bell Ltd

Why join a penitential crowd
where waters wind their sluggish way,
where prophet-like the Baptist stood
against the evil of his day?

Why hear the preaching of a man,
a honey eating, ragged rogue,
who fed on locusts and cajoled
the people on that desert road?

He spoke of God as one who knew
the essence of almighty law;
he taught with courage, lined with thought,
as though conviction made him sure.

The common people heard his call
to gather near the water's shroud,
and quietly, humbly, last of all,
see Jesus join that thronging crowd.

Messiah, Saviour, Lord or King,
whatever name he came to bear;
this moment he was one with them,
their turning point he came to share.

And what of us, what saps our praise?
Will intellect or power rob?
Or are we simply just too proud
to stand beside the Son of God?

© 2002 Stainer & Bell Ltd

Metre: LM

Written 20 November 1998

A Methodist Local Preacher, Susan Stewart, commented on the scarcity of hymns dealing with the baptism of Jesus. This was written in response.

George F. Bexon (1958–)

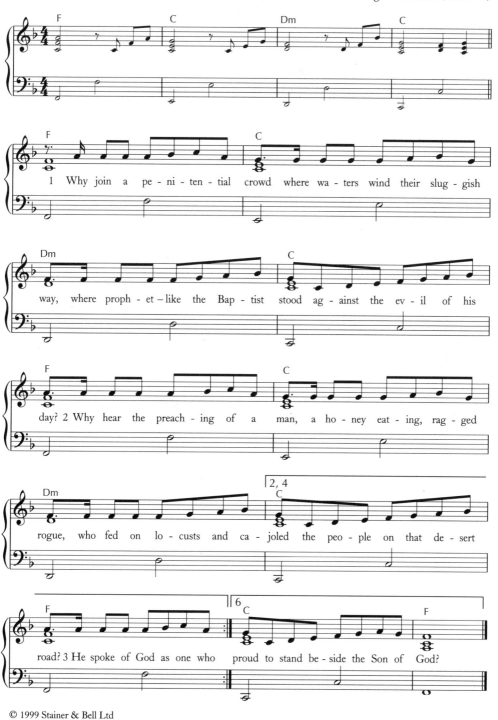

© 1999 Stainer & Bell Ltd

Why join a large and noisy crowd
where Jordan winds its sluggish way,
where prophet-like the Baptist stood
against the evil of his day?

Why hear the preaching of a man,
a honey eating, ragged rogue,
who fed on locusts and called out
to people on that desert road?

He spoke of God as one who knew
the sense of each and every law;
he taught with courage and with thought,
with every word he sounded sure.

The young and old they heard his call
to gather near the river side,
and quietly, humbly, last of all,
see Jesus join that human tide.

Messiah, Saviour, Lord or King,
whatever name he came to bear;
this moment he was one with them,
their turning point he came to share.

© 1999 Stainer & Bell Ltd

Metre: LM

Suggested Tune: This is sung to the same tune as the previous hymn *(see page 59)*, with a
suitable alteration to the ending of the last verse.

Written 20 November 1998

An alternative form of the previous text, for children.

George F. Bexon (1958–)

Look beyond where laser beams
sear the sky with shafts of green;
God is not beyond the stars,
God's close, if yet unseen!

As the shuttle soars through space
we may never touch God's face;
not a million miles away,
for God is in this place.

When the silver shoal surrounds
or we tunnel underground,
we are no more near to God,
for God is all around.

God is here, by you each day,
near you when you work or play,
there's no need to seek God out:
our God is here to stay!

Words and Music © 1999 Stainer & Bell Ltd

Metre: 7 7.7.6.

Written 27 October 1998

Written for 'Sound Bytes'. God is everywhere, and to discover divinity we don't need to go beyond where laser beams shaft across the sky. 'Silver shoal' refers to fish seen when diving.

BIRABUS

Peter Cutts (1937–)

Hid - den God,   I long to see___ you,   long___
___   to hear your voice;   here a - mid   the haste and
hur - ry,   need a rea - son to re - joice.

© 1974 Stainer & Bell Ltd for the world except USA and Canada

Hidden God, I long to see you,
long to hear your voice;
here amid the haste and hurry,
need a reason to rejoice.

More than just this global grounding,
more than just a home,
far beyond the raging river,
far beyond this fazing foam.

Blinding light of realisation,
long to catch a trace;
source, and end, of contemplation,
long to sense your saving grace.

But, if I should never glimpse you
help me to go on;
give me hope and motivation
still to sing with heaven's song.

© 1999 Stainer & Bell Ltd

Metre: 8.5.8.7.

Written 27 November 1998

It can be hard to keep faith when the presence of God is not obvious.

Harassed, haunted child of Mary
ran before he learned to crawl;
filled with horror, those who loved him,
those who gave to him their all,
tore him from his bed and birth place,
blown before the sudden squall.

Doubt and danger dogged each footfall,
normal sounds now raised their fear;
noises in a cobbled courtyard:
Herod's minions drawing near?
Or the waking sounds of morning?
Nothing now is safe or clear.

Out of this endangered childhood,
rootless, no asylum found,
grew the strength of God to greatness,
yet with thorns his brow was crowned:
clothes divided, scourged, derided,
suffering without a sound.

Dare we beautify the image
when Christ's heirs still walk this earth,
when our children, harassed, hounded,
suffer death before their birth,
while their parents' haunted hunger
speaks of their discarded worth?

© 2000 Stainer & Bell Ltd

Metre: 8.7.8.7.8.7.

Suggested Tunes: NEW MALDEN and PICARDY

Written 28 November 1998

Refugees are not new to the world, and children still suffer, as did Jesus.

Almighty God has done great things,
an angel proffers stunning news,
the news of human hope he brings,
her baby heaven and earth shall fuse;
and she will give her life for that,
O, Mary, sing magnificat.

A mother and her unborn child,
a man who ought to let her go
to save his face, stay undefiled,
as love and duty taunt and flow;
and Joseph will consider that
as Mary sings magnificat.

And all the greatness of a God,
distilled to love, sets captives free,
a single liberating Word:
those born in darkness now can see;
as human power considers that
let Mary sing magnificat.

© 2001 Stainer & Bell Ltd

Metre: 8.8.8.8.8.8.

Suggested Tune: MELITA

Written 22 December 1998

It is difficult to encapsulate the revolutionary sense of the Magnificat in hymns which are singable. Timothy Dudley-Smith and Fred Kaan have both written texts on this theme. Here is another!

The text was first sung as a solo by Anne Jarrett (who also features as a composer in this book) at a Christmas service in the Orrell and Lamberhead Green Circuit of the British Methodist Church, 2001.

How can people praise the Godhead,
save in humble penitence?
How can we avoid the verdict
of these years' indifference?
If our God has come among us
then we have betrayed a call;
out of selfish pride our grasping
puts our gain ahead of all.

If that God was born among us
then the people of that birth
suffered taunting and derision,
persecution on this earth.
Driven from their given cradle,
scattered seeds upon the wind;
Christians led that desecration
and, we wonder, will it end?

Holocaust, crusades, apartheid,
inquisition, slavery,
all have had a Christian presence,
justifying butchery;
every century adds locations
pictured on a map or chart,
scenes of human devastation,
hatred honed, become an art.

Now we stand and, just like Peter,
we've no cause to strut or crow,
we are self-deceived if claiming
righteousness, our debts you know:
debts of love we owe each other,
debts we never can repay;
for two thousand years' denial
Lord forgive, for this we pray.

Enter rooms of desolation,
bring your love to cleanse, to spare;
'Peace be with you', once you uttered,
let us hear and let us share;
bring us from this darkest moment
into dazzling, gleaming light,
may the blaze of this millennium
end the horror of our night.

© 2001 Stainer & Bell Ltd

Metre: 8.7.8.7.D.

Suggested Tunes: MANOR HOUSE and GENEVA

Written 1999

A reflection on the millennium. Published in 'Worship Live' No. 21.

Sound Bytes: words that stay in your head,
what Jesus did, the things he said.
Sound Bytes: words that stay in your head,
get on your feet, pick up your bed.

Tough words, words so neat,
counter the culture, stay on your feet.
God spoke, out in the night:
'let there be light', the world looks bright.
Good News! News for the poor,
the world is waiting, go through that door.
Go then, out to the world,
go with God, with love unfurled.

Sound Bytes: words that stay in your head,
what Jesus did, the things he said.
Sound Bytes: words that stay in your head,
do what he did, say what he said.

© 1999 Stainer & Bell Ltd

Metre: Irregular

Written 3 March 1999

In 1998 I was asked by Stainer & Bell to edit their new song book for schools, churches and junior churches, 'Sound Bytes', and this song was written in response to their invitation.

SOUND BYTES

Craig McLeish (1963–)

© 1999 Stainer & Bell Ltd

KOSOVO

Andrew Pratt (1948–)

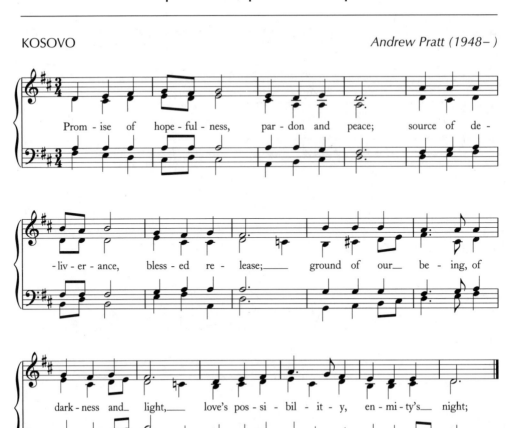

Prom - ise of hope - ful - ness, par - don and peace; source of de -
-liv - er - ance, bless - ed re - lease;___ ground of our___ be - ing, of
dark - ness and__ light,___ love's pos - si - bil - it - y, en - mi - ty's__ night;

© 2002 Stainer & Bell Ltd

Promise of hopefulness, pardon and peace;
source of deliverance, blessed release;
ground of our being, of darkness and light,
love's possibility, enmity's night;

Cleave to the centre of selfish desire
bring to creation by earth, wind or fire
all that is hoped for and all that's unseen:
goodness and glory are more than a dream.

In our absurdity, clamour and war
unseat our certainty, counter and floor
all sense of prejudice, hatred and then
offer us strangers that we can befriend.

Give us the courage to enter this cleft,
healing the hurt of the lost, the bereft,
offering hope, though our love's crucified,
soaking up malice where peace is denied;

Love is the answer to vengeance and wrath,
going on loving in spite of the loss,
facing the depth of depravity's gain,
burning our hatred on love's sweeter flame.

Pour out your spirit, God, fill up our lives,
offering loveliness, love that survives,
then take and lift us and raise up our song:
love is yet greater than all human wrong.

© 1999 Stainer & Bell Ltd

Metre: 10 10.10 10. Dactylic

Written 1 May 1999

Inspired by 'God, Jesus and Life in the Spirit' by David E. Jenkins, a former Bishop of Durham. First sung at a service which took place on 23 May 1999 at Kingsleigh Methodist Church in the Leigh and Hindley Circuit, to focus on the war in Kosovo.

LOVING CUP

Andrew Pratt (1948–)

Saw a bush with fi - ery leaves, heard a voice like God;
thought that this was spec - ial ground where his feet had trod.

(Moses)
Saw a bush with fiery leaves,
heard a voice like God;
thought that this was special ground
where his feet had trod.

(Isaiah)
Saw the temple filled with smoke,
awe-struck, he stood still,
felt that he had heard a call:
'Go and do God's will'.

(Jeremiah)
Like the clay the potter threw
was the life he owned,
twisted, moulded yet again,
till God was enthroned.

(Ezekiel)
Coloured visions shone and gleamed,
crystals spun with light,
God was near, not far away,
no more hid from sight.

(The Emmaus Road)
Walking down a winding road,
talking, yet in grief;
but when bread was broken, shared,
God brought them belief.

Words © 2000 and Music © 2002 Stainer & Bell Ltd

Metre: 7.5.7.5.

Written 9 May 1999

A sequence of biblical epiphanies. We can often find God in ordinary things.

LIEBSTER IMMANUEL

Himmels-Lust (1679 Jena)
arranged Peter Cutts (1937–)

From all that's bleak___ and un - for - giv - ing, e - vad - ing

hope, de - ny - ing___ liv - ing; from deep des - pair I

call to you; but___ can___ you___ hear, O God?

Arrangement © 2002 Stainer & Bell Ltd for the world except USA and Canada

From all that's bleak and unforgiving,
evading hope, denying living;
from deep despair I call to you;
but can you hear, O God?

O hear my voice, my pleading, praying,
for your free grace I'm hoping, waiting;
for when you count each fault I bear,
how can I stand, O God?

More than the watch that waits for morning,
of steadfast love I seek the dawning,
your mercy is my only hope;
I wait and trust, O God.

© 2002 Stainer & Bell Ltd

Metre: 9 9.8.6.

Written 4 June 1999

Psalm 130 inspired this text.

God is your source of strength and help,
ground of this changing, cosmic scheme;
you need not look beyond the hills,
God folds you close in love unseen.

God never sleeps by day or night,
God's love will never lose its grip;
your God will never let you down,
your foot will never slide or slip.

The hottest sun will bring no harm,
nor will the moon bring hurt or fear
for God has guarded you with care,
and love will always hold you near.

Each journey that you make in life,
your coming in, your going out,
will show how much God loves you still,
through every danger, fear or doubt.

© 2002 Stainer & Bell Ltd

Metre: LM

Suggested Tunes: EDEN and WOODWORTH

Written 4 June 1999

Recent metrical interpretations of Psalm 121 have clung closely to the familiar Scottish paraphrase. This text is offered as an alternative.

61 When anger is our highest creed

When anger is our highest creed,
revenge the motivating force;
God, understand our depth of hurt,
our need for action, not just thought.

Ejected from what makes us safe,
familiar ground and well-known names,
we sicken for the things we've seen,
all sense of hope and courage drains.

We cannot celebrate our faith,
and faith lacks meaning, all is lost;
for nothing is as it once was,
we cannot ever bear the cost.

So, God, what should we do or say?
What is there left of love or life?
What mitigating cause or plea
will rid us of this pain of strife?

Amid our sense of grief and loss
where nothing now can be the same,
stand in the midst of shattered faith;
rebuild, renew, and raise again.

© 2001 Stainer & Bell Ltd

Metre: LM

Suggested Tunes: PLAISTOW and KEDRON

Written 5 June 1999

Inspired by Psalm 137, and reflecting on the place of the refugee in this and every time.

O Source of many cultures,
of lives, beliefs and faith;
you brought us all together
to share one world in space;
> Now show us how to honour
> each vision of your way,
> to live within the tension
> of difference you display.

The colour and the culture,
that kept us both apart,
are gifts that we can offer,
a means for us to start
> a journey with each other,
> till hand in hand we show,
> through mutual understanding,
> respect and love can grow.

© 2000 Stainer & Bell Ltd

Metre: 7.6.7.6.D.

Suggested Tunes: KING'S LYNN and AURELIA

Written 20 July 1999

Texts on the theme of reconciliation have become even more necessary since the destruction of the World Trade Center in New York on 11 September 2001. People must work and worship together, with those of other faiths and beliefs, and with an understanding that we share a common parenthood in God. Written on returning from Leyton in East London and reading in Genesis 29 the story of Jacob, Laban, Leah and Rachel. Originally the text began: 'O God of many cultures'. I hope the amendment might add to its inclusivity.

63 Friend of the world, bright shining sun!

Friend of the world, bright shining sun!
Reeling and dancing, life begun;
living and learning, climbing high,
soaring on wings as if to fly.

Friend of the ones we would despise,
fierce is the love within his eyes;
fierce in defence of poor or weak,
he offers love when we just speak.

Autumn is coming to the trees,
colour is drained from falling leaves;
darkness is covering all the earth,
his dance goes on, it finds new birth.

© 1999 Stainer & Bell Ltd

Metre: LM

Suggested Tunes: MARYTON and HURSLEY

Written 26 August 1999

This text, used as a dedication to 'Sound Bytes', was first sung at the funeral of my son Jonathan, and was written within twelve hours of his death on 25 August 1999.

Now we know there is a season
for the things we do on earth,
and behind each act a reason
for that time to come to birth.

Stones are gathered, stones are scattered,
wisdom watches all we do,
now we're dancing, now we're mourning,
life is changing, each day new.

People born and people dying,
trees are planted, woods torn down,
armies gather, sick of killing,
seek for healing, peace their crown.

Broken now the things we valued,
novel visions we will trace;
gone the things we thought for keeping,
held, what now stands in their place.

We have searched, the search is ended,
what was torn it's time to mend;
we must know what to dispose of
and the things we must commend.

Now it's time to keep our silence,
words enough have been set free,
hatred now must die forever,
love determine all we see.

© 2000 Stainer & Bell Ltd

Metre: 8.7.8.7. Trochaic

Suggested Tunes: STUTTGART and GALILEE

Written 9 September 1999

Ecclesiastes 3:1–8, read at my son's funeral by my niece, Hannah, was brought to my mind again by a recording of The Byrds singing 'Turn, turn, turn'.

65 Is buried faith now dead?

Is buried faith now dead,
or can it quietly grow?
As grief matures within each heart,
we never can let go.

The body that we loved
is hidden from our sight:
no hand to hold, no lips to kiss,
no laughter to delight;

But, as the days grow short,
and as the seasons pass,
they say the things that once were sharp
may soften to our grasp,

that what we hold will last,
that faith, perhaps, will grow
like snowdrops under frozen ground
that penetrate the snow.

But, as the years drift down,
death still retains its sting.
our faith has changed, love runs as deep,
words have a hollow ring.

© 2002 Stainer & Bell Ltd

Metre: SM

Suggested Tunes: GARELOCHSIDE and BOYLSTON

Written 10 September 1999

A commentary on maturing grief.

Seed and sign of all creation
cradled in her parents' arms;
child of hope and exaltation,
all our selfishness disarms.

God has trusted us with keeping
this new life, to watch her grow;
care for her when waking, sleeping,
then to watch her freely go.

May our loving be abundant
so that she may thrive and live,
so that fear may be redundant;
as God gave, so let us give.

© 2002 Stainer & Bell Ltd

Metre: 8.7.8.7. Trochaic

Suggested Tunes: HALTON HOLGATE and FOR THE BREAD

Written 11 September 1999

For Elizabeth, and for her parents, Ann and Steven.

The cosmic pulse that beats through all creation,
two spinning stars, the pulsar's throbbing light;
these wing beats, not a passing aberration,
but angels thronging through the mists of night;

The whirling, dancing, trance that brings relation
with all that is and all that is to be;
the mystic, magic prayer, this wild elation
you say will bring the love to set us free;

Our language cannot offer a description:
Nirvana, heaven, call it what you will;
this other world that fires our inspiration
is all that conjures up the power to thrill.

The god we hymn, through praise and acclamation,
we seek to meet through words or bread and wine;
yet all the world inspires your incantation;
together let us fathom truth's design.

© 2002 Stainer & Bell Ltd

Metre: 11.10.11.10. Iambic

Suggested Tune: INTERCESSOR

Written 24 October 1999

Reading about Pagan (but not satanic) religion, in which my son had an interest, I have been struck not only by its apparent pantheism, but also its nearness to Christian mysticism. This text follows on from these reflections, and expresses a hope that all those who seek God and the betterment of humanity may be united in that common quest.

Christ saw a way so clearly
that others feared to tread;
with those who were discarded
he deigned to rest his head.

The poor he suffered gladly,
at hypocrites he'd rant;
his vision was not clouded
by sanctimonious cant.

He died, but still those faces
look on with mild disgust;
naivety that's guileless,
the flaw they could not trust.

He'll whirl and dance before them,
his song will fill the air;
we'll join the dance he started,
in spite of our despair;

For he has spun a rainbow
of singing, shining light;
his leap to love and freedom
defies the darkest night.

© 2002 Stainer & Bell Ltd

Metre: 7.6.7.6. Iambic

Suggested Tune: CHRISTUS DER IST MEIN LEBEN

Written 10 October 1999

Jesus chose a way of life that others would shun. In his own way my son did the same, befriending homeless people and living alongside them. For a father that is hard to watch but, at the same time, challenging. Ultimately, in Christian understanding, Jesus went through death to resurrection and light. My son, who mixed Christianity and scientific cosmology with pagan religion and crystal healing, was killed in an accident.

WENTWORTH   Peter Cutts (1937–)

How can we con-fine God____ with-in our mind, held____

____ with-in a creed____ hu-man-ly de-signed?

© 2002 Stainer & Bell Ltd for the world except USA and Canada

How can we confine
God within our mind,
held within a creed
humanly designed?

Surely such a joy
cannot be contained
by a single plan,
humanly explained?

How can we be sure
that the way we know
is the only path
that this God might show?

People of all faiths
let us all conspire;
source and ground of life
answer our desire.

As we long to know
answers to our plight,
take us, lead our quest,
dancing to the light.

© 2002 Stainer & Bell Ltd

Metre: 5.5.5.5.

Written 7 November 1999

It has been said that the way to so great a gift as God must be more than singular. I do not believe that any single faith has the monopoly of truth. Another text for people of different faiths to sing together.

On a Galilean hillside
stood a crowd with wondering eyes,
captivated by the mystery,
framed by mountain, sea and skies.

Jesus stood, and with compassion,
met their gaze and understood
depth of pain, and human anguish,
evil challenging their good.

What he said defied their senses,
challenged values, yet affirmed
those whom life had spurned or battered,
lifted them above the herd.

Now we stand, impassioned, waiting
for a word to cure our ill;
but he challenges complacence,
love is ours to share or still.

© 2002 Stainer & Bell Ltd

Metre: 8.7.8.7. Trochaic

Suggested Tunes: WRAYSBURY and GALILEE

Written 8 November 1999

My son is buried between the sea and the mountains on the North Wales coast. In reverie I imagined Galilee.

In a room of quiet seclusion,
Jesus sharing bread and wine.
Was this just some strange illusion:
talk of branches of one vine?

Such idyllic separation,
from the world of stress and strife,
soon was countered by confusion
devastating love and life.

Judas innocently asking
who would speak the fatal word;
bread and wine he went on sharing
with this Jesus, known as 'Lord'.

All integrity was threatened
as the silver bought a kiss,
as injustice blindly blundered
into such a world as this;

And that kiss so coolly proffered,
calm betrayal echoes still,
as each crisp deception offered
lights a contrast to God's will.

There is no secure seclusion
from the pressures of the world,
from the conflict of creation,
where deception is not heard.

Can one branch betray another;
damn, disown; at what a price?
Each should seek to greet the other:
nurture, shield, encourage life.

© 2000 Stainer & Bell Ltd

Metre: 8.7.8.7. Trochaic

Suggested Tunes: HALTON HOLGATE and EMMAUS

Written 2000

The church is pictured as branches of a vine, which is God. Yet the church is visibly divided.

This love, this life, this enterprise
is that by which we will arise
affirmed, up-raised, to live again
when we have suffered death or pain.

Our practical adventure here
involves both urgency and care;
compelled by shared humanity
to offer love, set people free.

And if the task enlarges sight
to wider visions, greater height
than those which we can reach on earth,
then know that God has come to birth.

© 2002 Stainer & Bell Ltd

Metre: LM

Suggested Tunes: INVITATION and CANONBURY

Written 12 January 2000

Written after I read 'The Sea of Faith' by Don Cupitt, this text explores the idea that God is made present in our actions.

When I'm driven, never resting,
senses numb and colours merge
leaving life devoid of meaning,
lost within this senseless surge.

Time collapses; moments, fleeting,
pass before I've time to count.
All that mattered in my searching
turns to tension, stress and doubt.

Give me value, end this chasing
after dreams that fade so fast.
Touch me with your gentle laughter,
give me joy and love to last.

Help me find a way from darkness
to the light of calm and peace;
then within your warmth and comfort,
love give rest, let striving cease.

© 2002 Stainer & Bell Ltd

Metre: 8.7.8.7. Trochaic

Suggested Tune: SICILIAN MARINERS

Written 17 January 2000

A plea for personal peace.

The force of love will not be stilled:
peace, it never comes easily;
in love of life we should be skilled:
peace, it never comes easily.
Peacemakers, young and old, must come
and work for peace till peace is won.

Let's offer each the hand of peace:
peace, it never comes easily;
let's sing and pray for love's release:
peace, it never comes easily.
We'll offer all we have and more
to pledge to put an end to war.

We'll live our lives, if need be die:
peace, it never comes easily;
we'll walk, we'll write, we'll dance, we'll cry:
peace, it never comes easily.
We'll live and love and pray for peace,
and know this work must never cease.

© 2000 Stainer & Bell Ltd

Metre: 8.8.8.8.8 8.

Suggested Tune: SUSSEX CAROL

Written 19 January 2000

This hymn was completed in April 2000 for the Methodist Peace Fellowship, and published in 'Peace Makers & Dream Wakers'. Use of the tune 'Sussex Carol' requires a slight adjustment of the musical rhythm to fit lines two and four.

The pathway to peace will lead us through pain.
This will not dissuade, our love will remain.
We'll value our neighbours, bring wealth to the poor,
we'll break down each barrier, each wall and each door;

This pathway we'll claim of love and concern,
we'll talk and we'll listen so we may learn
the way from indifference, compassion's decree,
the manner of pardon, the way to be free.

We'll greet the oppressed, may prejudice cease;
one world, that's our prayer through justice and peace,
yet not in some heaven, beyond reach or hope,
but here on this planet, within human scope.

© 2000 Stainer & Bell Ltd

Metre: 10 10.11 11.

Suggested Tunes: TETHERDOWN and STANLEY BEACH

Written 19 January 2000

Completed in April 2000 for the Methodist Peace Fellowship, and published in 'Peace Makers & Dream Wakers'. Peace-making is, invariably, a painful affair.

Warm is the word we shall speak to our neighbour,
offering the love that has come from the heart.
Bridges we're building to span gulfs of hatred;
now is the time we must make a new start.

Follies have threatened our task from the outset,
words have been shallow and actions misplaced.
Help us to listen with care to our neighbour,
then may our answers disarm by their grace.

Let us avow by our words and intentions
never to stultify love at its source,
but by our dialogue, here and hereafter,
always to value and never to force.

Let our demeanour confront each division
built by tradition or fathered by hate;
let us continue to break down dissension,
working in hope, and not governed by fate.

© 2000 Stainer & Bell Ltd

Metre: 11.10.11.10. Dactylic

Suggested Tunes: QUEDLINBURG and WAS LEBET

Written 19 January 2000

Written in response to a request by David Harding, a retired British Methodist Minister and hymn-writer, for a text on the subject of peace. I believe that peace will only come through action and conflict resolution which admit to divisions and work to overcome them. Published in 'Peace Makers & Dream Wakers', where verse 4 appeared as follows:

Then as we utter each fond acclamation,
joined as if sisters and brothers from birth,
let us continue to break down dissension,
working for peace and renewal on earth.

77   Will you use imagination?

Will you use imagination
when you comfort those who grieve,
being open to their heartache,
casting off all you believe?

Will you climb their awful mountain,
filled with anguished tears of dread?
Will your Isaac walk beside you,
will your hand caress his head?

Will imagination wander
over things that you have shared,
as the path becomes yet steeper,
as the native rock is bared?

Now that rock is harsh and barren,
all of love has drained away;
death has entered uninvited,
dawn will not re-wake this day.

Not for you release or wonder;
there's no thicket, there's no ram;
just the consequential anguish,
can you square this with God's plan?

All the love received or given,
all the pain that you have born,
seems as nothing in the darkness
of this heedless, squalid morn.

If the faith that now lies buried
ever is to live again,
it must pass to love from anguish
through this vale of bitter pain.

© 2001 Stainer & Bell Ltd

Metre: 8.7.8.7. Trochaic

Suggested Tunes: ADORATION (Hunt) and CHARLESTOWN

Written 16 February 2000

There is no easy way out of grief. The only way back to life is through it. Much talk of resurrection addressed to those who are grieving can sound like platitude. I wanted to explore this through the imagery of the story of Abraham and Isaac, and by taking the narrative to its anticipated, though non-biblical, conclusion.

The dance of love is in our bones,
it gives life purpose, shape and form,
it challenges our vast concerns
and questions each deceptive norm.

This cosmic dance inflames each star
and gives the supernova light,
it fashions ethics and informs
each human thought, each human right.

This dance, the universal force,
that brings all living art to be,
will never cease or lose its power,
this ground of loving certainty.

© 2002 Stainer & Bell Ltd

Metre: LM

Suggested Tune: DUNEDIN

Written 25 February 2000

The 'dance' here equates with the logos (John 1) that permeates creation.

When song gives way to solitude,
and loneliness conspires with fear;
when walls of anguish tower around,
and agony is sharp and shear;
deep in the midst of our concern
love can, love must, love will draw near.

When all is dark and comfortless
and no one near can hear our sighs,
when tears are salt with bitterness
and all we know are jeers and lies;
here in the midst of our despair
love shares our pain and with us cries.

When all is seared with grief and loss
and faith seems empty or absurd,
when life lacks purpose, shape or form,
we find no sense, we frame no word;
here in the furnace of our fear
love whispers peace and will be heard.

© 2002 Stainer & Bell Ltd

Metre: 8.8.8.8.8.8.

Suggested Tune: OLD 112TH/VATER UNSER

Written 25 February 2000

In deepest grief love can remain, and though we might doubt the image we previously held of God, the 'still small voice' may continue to be heard.

When need and necessity no longer knock,
each minute seems endless, so endlessly slow;
when all we have left is the tedium of days
with no one to see and still nowhere to go.

When watching and waiting is all that there is,
and hope is a memory, a past we once knew;
when love is deception, and life seems to die,
the friends that we cherished so sparse and so few;

O what is our task as we wait out the years,
just what is the purpose of living and strife,
as here in the desert we linger each day?
O love, give a reason, a meaning for life.

© 2002 Stainer & Bell Ltd

Metre: 11.11.11.11.

Suggested Tunes: DATCHET and AWAY IN A MANGER

Written 27 February 2000

A reflection on how we may become increasingly isolated as age and infirmity take their toll. The American tune 'Away in a manger' provides an ironic feel. So often in age we return to those hymns and tunes we remember best.

Was the wilderness like this:
barren, purposeless and bleak;
void of all that matters most,
all that fills the words we speak?

O to hear that inner voice,
voice of challenge or of care;
but the silence shouts out loud,
deadens all that might be there.

Words describe each sight and sound,
all that stands outside ourselves;
but the gulf that lies within,
that's where desolation dwells.

Then a child-like cry rings out:
filled with solitary fear,
all the loneliness of life,
as our deepest grief draws near:

Here is where we stand alone
with no hand to hold or guide.
Could a still, small voice be heard?
Could it be we cannot hide?

Grief at what we understand,
what we never understood,
death of neighbour, death of self,
death of what we once called God.

Pain of love is all we know,
love in all its depth and sense;
God forsaken here we hang,
pay our part of love's expense.

© 2002 Stainer & Bell Ltd

Metre: 7.7.7.7.

Suggested Tunes: REBECCA and INNOCENTS

Written 6 March 2000

The risk of loving is the risk of losing. When we lose someone by death or separation, it may be that nothing can assuage our grief. The text explores such a sense of desolation.

Where mines are capped and mills have closed,
where commerce cannot make a mark,
come Spirit of the living God,
bring life in darkness, flame and spark.

Amid the city tenements,
or on a heathered Pennine slope,
look out, look up, and see the light
that freezes fear, that raises hope.

Along canal or river bank,
by road, by metro-link or rail,
this multi-cultured interface
may love inform, let love prevail.

© 2000 Stainer & Bell Ltd

Metre: LM

Suggested Tune: BRESLAU

Written 6 April 2000

Written for the Bolton and Rochdale District of the British Methodist Church and published in the 'Methodist Recorder', 11 May 2000. In the first verse, 'commerce' originally read 'dot-com'.

Where industry has come and gone,
where commerce cannot make a mark,
come Spirit of the living God,
bring life in darkness, flame and spark.

Amid Manhattan's high-rise blocks,
or on an Appalachian slope,
look out, look up, and see the light
that freezes fear, that raises hope.

Away out West or in the East,
by air, by freeway or by rail,
this multi-cultured interface
may love inform, let love prevail.

© 2002 Stainer & Bell Ltd

Metre: LM

Suggested Tune: BRESLAU

Amended 25 January 2002

The previous text, 'Where mines are capped and mills have closed', amended for the USA.

We come by many different paths,
each certain that our way is true.
As sisters, brothers, let us talk,
a way to peace is overdue.
Caged in a creed, we think we've caught
the source of all that is to be,
but God cannot be thus confined:
the Spirit's flying, wild and free!

We think that we alone have found
the secret goal of all the earth;
we make our rules, oppress the weak,
with shackles hold them from their birth.
Within four walls we idolise
the treasures of our certainty.
We worship all that we have made.
Outside God sits in poverty.

So, prophets of this present age
disturb us in our arrogance
to let the Spirit freely blow,
to offer love's extravagance.
For love can shake our self-conceit,
tear up each creed, each guarantee;
confronting cant and human pride,
God demonstrates love's quality.

© 2002 Stainer & Bell Ltd

Metre: DLM

Suggested Tunes: LONDON (KETTERING) and HE LEADETH ME

Written 19 May 2000

The original version of this text was written in response to a request for a hymn for a service uniting two Anglican churches. Originally the churches had been a Mother and a Daughter. Now they were to come together as equals. The text would be equally useful in ecumenical or certain inter-faith contexts.

LITHE SPIRIT

Andrew Pratt (1948–)

Lithe spir-it you're bound-ing and leap-ing,_____ stars
shim-mer and flash from your heels,_____ un-til the whole world burns with
par-don and praise, un-til the lost know how love feels._____

O harlequin dazzle by dancing,
let joy spring like sparks from a flame,
until every person consumed by your love
comes blithely to join in your game.

Come juggler, spinning and turning
our chances and dreams like a top,
until all our values are turned upside down
whirl on through the world, never stop.

Words and Music © 2002 Stainer & Bell Ltd

Metre: 9.8.11.8.

Written 21 May 2000

This text, following Sydney Carter, uses the metaphors of dance and the harlequin to represent God. Additionally, I have chosen to use the juggler. First sung at Pentecost 2002 in Bispham Methodist Church in the Orrell Lamberhead Green Circuit with a dance by Sarah Neal and Jessica Cuerdon.

Holy anger, blazing outrage,
force that never will be stilled;
always thirsting after justice
till each need has been fulfilled
demonstrates our Christian passion,
fired by deep prophetic grace,
reaching to the heart of violence
till each fear has been effaced.

Here compassion finds its centre,
rooted in our parent God;
feeling pain in isolation,
walking where the anguished trod,
holding on when all seems hopeless,
we can never love enough;
yet resisting each oppressor
though the way is steep and rough.

When the faulted, flawed and vanquished
found in trauma they were free,
then they buried dangerous memories,
precious hopes of what can be.
We must reach beyond oppression,
past the memories of our dead
through the phantoms and repression
of the words we've left unsaid.

Here the seeds of recreation
struggle in unfriendly ground,
struggle in the darkened silence,
for their history to be found.
Love is sown in our experience
where all joy has ceased to dwell;
searching for the shafting sunlight,
finding hope within this hell.

© 2002 Stainer & Bell Ltd

Metre: 8.7.8.7.D.

Suggested Tunes: EBENEZER and IN BABILONE

Written 16 June 2000

It has been suggested that societal memories, dangerous memories, can be a source of strength in times of testing. I am indebted to Jan Hicks for bringing this concept to my attention.

I feel amid this calm despair
an inner voice, confounding sense,
that whispers love, that offers choice;
that counters my belligerence.

Beyond my caged, enquiring mind,
transcendent yet uniquely near,
it penetrates my enmity
and counters every fault and fear.

This source of all imagining
orgasmic source of stars and lights
confronts my infant prejudice
exploding doubt, new hope ignites.

© 2002 Stainer & Bell Ltd

Metre: LM

Suggested Tune: MARYTON

Written 26 July 2000

Written in Boston USA at the Conference of the Hymn Society in the United States and Canada. People often refer to God as an inner voice, which in this text offers hope amid despair.

This goal of equality laid out before us,
where each one is valued and no-one denied,
is given, through loving, to those who will listen,
yet, while we should welcome, we often deride.

We look at our neighbours and judge by appearance:
the colour of skin or the cadence of voice,
the cut of a jacket or youthful confusion,
while prejudice beckons our ultimate choice.

Yet love would compel to see Christ clothe our neighbour,
the ragged and ugly gain elegant grace;
enabling discernment, refined understanding:
the future is present and all have a place.

© 2001 Stainer & Bell Ltd

Metre: 12.11.12.11.

Suggested Tunes: ST CATHERINE'S COURT and KREMSER

Written 26 July 2000

Written in Boston USA at the Conference of the Hymn Society in the United States and Canada. A reflection on the ideals of the Constitution of the United States and the way in which humanly we strive to meet such ideals but never quite make it. So it is with God's goal for humanity.

What would wonder hold before us?
All the pride of God on earth?
Yet in deep humiliation
here a child had come to birth.
Through the dark of that cold stable
not an angel sought to sing;
not a shepherd, wise or stupid,
had a lamb that he could bring.

Not a jewel, not Edom's odour,
not a single star-filled shower
broke upon that sullen stillness
fracturing its silent power.
Yet another birth had happened,
but millennia have passed
since this archetype of heartache
brought creation to its fast.

All this time has added mystery,
truth is glazed with hope or fear
by the years' interpretation,
fact no longer sure or clear.
So we speculate and tamper
with a simple sordid birth,
birth within a darkened stable:
God, despised, in flesh on earth.

© 2001 Stainer & Bell Ltd

Metre: 8.7.8.7.D.

Suggested Tunes: PLEADING SAVIOUR and BEECHER

Written 30 July 2000

Theological interpretation led to the gospel record depicting the birth of Jesus in a particular way. We have built on this over the years until the scandal of the incarnation is lost in sentimentality. This text seeks to address the issue. I am not at all sure that Jesus's birth was as pretty as we have painted it.

90   On the sidewalk, by the shop-front

RECONCILIATION

Hal H. Hopson (1933–)

On the side-walk, by the shop-front I laid down my mat to sleep; tears of sad-ness welled with-in me, thoughts of all that might have been. we may cope.

© 2000 Hope Publishing Company, Carol Stream, IL 60188, USA. (Administered in UK by CopyCare, PO Box 77, Hailsham BN27 3EF, UK, music@copycare.com.) All rights reserved. Used by permission.

On the sidewalk, by the shop-front
I laid down my mat to sleep;
tears of sadness welled within me,
thoughts of all that might have been.

Lost within this hidden city
where the subway hums and groans,
left unnoticed and defenceless,
God forsaken and alone.

Can you sense my thrumming heart-beat,
can you feel a reason why
in your wealth you're just as lonely,
waiting for your time to die?

Maybe I should look more clearly
through the eyes of given hope,
maybe you could stoop more lowly
that together we may cope.

© 2002 Stainer & Bell Ltd

Metre: 8.7.8.7. Trochaic

Written 27 July 2000

Written in Boston USA at the Conference of the Hymn Society in the United States and Canada. The contrast between rich and poor is as evident in Boston as in any other Western city. The rhyme moves towards resolution while the sense of hope and relationship deepen as the text proceeds.

We welcome you into our midst,
a stranger, soon to be a friend;
we hope that you will feel at home,
that bonds, now formed, may never end.

As Jesus reached his hand to those
whose apprehension he could sense,
so here we pray, that Spirit filled,
you'll live with Christ-like confidence.

Now let us join in word and deed
the mission that we're called to share;
in fellowship by God we're bound
to offer love, hope, peace and care.

© 2001 Stainer & Bell Ltd

Metre: LM

Suggested Tunes: MARTHAM and GERMANY

Written 5 August 2000

Written for the welcome of the Rev. Sue Whitehead to the Leigh and Hindley Methodist Circuit. I was surprised and pleased when the Circuit Stewards of the Orrell and Lamberhead Green Circuit chose to use it at my own welcome service a year later.

We wait in praise and freedom,
both children of God's grace;
anticipating passion,
love in each other's face.

We seek the gift of insight,
in need of human care,
in hope, anticipating
the joy we long to share.

The partnership we marry,
the depth of faith we seal,
are witness to the knowledge
the love we have is real.

Then God please bless this union,
this meeting of two minds,
this fusion of two bodies,
with all that heaven finds.

© 2002 Stainer & Bell Ltd

Metre: 7.6.7.6. Iambic

Suggested Tunes: KNECHT and CHRISTUS DER IST MEIN LEBEN

Written 26 August 2000

My response to a request from Geoffrey Duncan for inclusive hymnody resulted in this hymn for a gay marriage. Published in the anthology 'Courage to Love'.

Through touching and loving our faithfulness grows,
we're drawn to each other, encouraged, love shows;
but even the depths of our human desire
are cold to the furnace of God's hidden fire.

In every relationship where we are known
some facets are covered and others are shown;
but God will enlighten, expose to our view,
a depth of compassion that we never knew.

So great is God's faithfulness, seasons of care
will merge with each other and endlessly share
the touch and the tenderness, love's strong embrace,
a sensual expression of consummate grace.

© 2002 Stainer & Bell Ltd

Metre: 11.11.11.11.

Suggested Tune: MINIVER

Written 28 August 2000

Written in response to a request for texts that would enable the celebration of same-sex relationships. The words could equally apply to a heterosexual relationship in which there was a willingness to acknowledge the God-given nature of sensuality. Published in the anthology 'Courage to Love'.

We praise you God for you have made
a world of such variety;
a world of colour, light and shade,
of varied sexuality.

We come as ones who love you, God,
in many different frames and ways.
Accept us, help us find a place
to share your loving, daring days.

We hold each other, hold us now
and never, ever let us go.
God, give us generosity
that we may share the love we know.

© 2002 Stainer & Bell Ltd

Metre: LM

Suggested Tunes: MELCOMBE and CANONBURY

Written 28 August 2000

Written in response to a request for a text that could be used to celebrate gay and lesbian sexuality. Published in the anthology 'Courage to Love'. Originally verse 2, line 3 read 'Indulge us, help us find a place'. This is an accepted alternative but it could raise the question, 'what need is there for God's indulgence when all that is required is the same acceptance as for anyone else?'

Where do I fit, what is my place,
amid my family and friends?
How can I keep integrity
with who I am, with what God sends?

What is my part within this frame
that holds a picture of the past:
a mother, father, sister, child;
where can I stand, what place will last?

One in a body bound by love:
my love for them, I hope they see.
Just as I am, accept me God.
Just as I am may they love me.

© 2002 Stainer & Bell Ltd

Metre: LM

Suggested Tunes: TALLIS' CANON and CORNISH

Written 28 August 2000

A text which asks the questions of one who feels on the outside, different, for whatever reason. Published in the anthology 'Courage to Love'.

Living in and out of glory;
paradox: incarnate God.
Brush-strokes filling out the story,
echoes of a world Christ trod.

Held within the gospel's danger,
etched, God's self-denying grace;
Jesus, loving saint and stranger,
met in every neighbour's face.

Down through years of imitation
running counter to that Word,
now our rude interpretation
makes our clamour more absurd.

Now in this day's generation,
as we raise our hands above,
giving praise for all creation,
at our feet God pleads for love.

© 2002 Stainer & Bell Ltd

Metre: 8.7.8.7. Trochaic

Suggested Tunes: LAUS DEO (REDHEAD 46) and FOR THE BREAD

Written 12 September 2000

We continue to witness to the paradox of the incarnation through our own lives and actions. Often what we do provides a flawed imitation of Jesus.

Come join the circle, share our song:
see shadows swirl and bodies sway,
as proud imagination fails
and strong men stand in mute dismay.

The spirit is for each and all:
we are no longer trodden down.
We'll sing and dance from dark till dawn
while donning laughter's smiling gown.

O sister God draw forth our cry:
no longer muffled, silenced, stilled.
Our shout must echo round the world:
your promise is at last fulfilled.

© 2002 Stainer & Bell Ltd

Metre: LM

Suggested Tunes: BROCKHAM and DUNEDIN

Written 3 November 2000

*'Strong men stand in mute dismay' (1 Samuel 2:4), suggested by the book 'Introducing a Practical
Feminist Theology of Worship' by Janet Wootton. Those who are oppressed, for whatever reason, can
lead the dance and the worship of God.*

She breathed through chaos, ordering creation.
She moulded virgin clay, brought life to birth.
She over-saw our human cultivation
of Eden, archetype of mother earth.

She energised Eve's eloquent discernment
enabling her debate and reason's choice.
She is the seat of human understanding
that leads us to lament or to rejoice.

She broods and births and nurtures expectation.
She is the source and goal of all that is.
Immersed in sadness, buoyed by exaltation,
beyond our living, yet in all that lives.

We celebrate the hope she holds before us:
death's fracture she has promised she will mend.
Our God, our mother, breathes a new beginning:
her love our ground, our life, our goal, our end.

© 2002 Stainer & Bell Ltd

Metre: 11.10.11.10. Iambic

Suggested Tune: INTERCESSOR

Written 9 November 2000

In 'Introducing a Practical Feminist Theology of Worship' Janet Wootton makes the point that 'wisdom' and 'spirit' in the Old Testament are feminine. Adam took the fruit of the tree of knowledge, but it was Eve who discerned intellectually what was on offer. This insight removes the negative association placed on Eve and uncovers a positive emphasis which has hitherto been hidden.

Is this drama: soaring wonder,
perfect prose, angelic strains,
singing silence, ringing thunder,
fitting worship God ordains?

Is this praising, contemplation,
empty ritual, hollow rite,
just tradition, forced elation,
or a feast of joy and light?

Is this sacramental sealing
just an action without heart,
or a cosmic source of healing,
through whose power we bear a part?

Are we kinder, more forgiving,
since we came to worship here?
Through our loving and our living
is the world less filled with fear?

Are our lives more fit for caring,
has our love a wider scope?
Are our neighbours less despairing,
are their lives more filled with hope?

For this God we claim to honour,
with pretentious pomp and pride,
shares derision and dishonour
with the ones we've shut outside.

© 2002 Stainer & Bell Ltd

Metre: 8.7.8.7. Trochaic

Suggested Tunes: GOTT WILL'S MACHEN and STUTTGART

Written 15 November 2000

Dedicated to Lionel Blue – the Radio Rabbi. All the wonder, the choral perfection, the sacramental precision in the world is nothing if at the end we are no better as people.

Here stands a stranger, who is she?
We do not know. Whom do we see,
someone who threatens you and me?
Is she a foe, or friend?

Here stands a person, young or old,
seeking asylum, so we're told.
How does he fit your frame or mould?
Is he your foe or friend?

Here stands a child: assess her need.
What should we offer so we heed
her cry of hunger, so we feed
this child? This foe? This friend?

Here stands a person, this time, you.
The choice is yours. What will you do
to ask this stranger in, or sue
this foe, who could be friend?

Here is a mirror, see your face.
What do you offer: hatred, grace,
now in this very time and place,
to Christ you call your friend.

© 2002 Stainer & Bell Ltd

Metre: 8 8 8.6.

Suggested Tune: MISERICORDIA

Written 26 November 2000

Written for the Christian Council for Racial Justice. The call to see Christ in others is testing.

The day will come, must come, and soon,
when we will sing a song of joy
with sisters, brothers, not like us,
who share the image of one God.

Whatever name, whichever faith,
at heart we share a common bond,
a shared humanity in God,
whose name and character is love.

That love will drive us to the day
when every wall is broken down,
when love and joy and song are one:
that day will come, must come, and soon.

© 2001 Stainer & Bell Ltd

Metre: LM

Suggested Tune: TALLIS' CANON

Written 28 January 2001

Written following the BBC 'Songs of Praise' Holocaust Memorial programme. In the twenty-first century it is ever more apparent that we need to learn how to live together respecting and even celebrating difference. We must worship together. Such an act is criticised as requiring belief to be reduced to a common denominator. Rather, it will push us towards a search for those things in common that really matter. The things that separate us will then be seen as of lesser significance. Ultimately they will not matter at all. Published in 'Worship Live' No. 21.

Though we understand the genome,
fathom depths of deepest space,
still we recognise our longing:
seeking love and needing grace.

Through unfathomable kindness,
breaching walls of fear and pride,
you have offered simple answers
that the arrogant deride.

Help us penetrate our blindness
to your love and to our need;
as we seek you, may you find us,
meeting us despite our greed.

© 2002 Stainer & Bell Ltd

Metre: 8.7.8.7. Trochaic

Suggested Tunes: WYCHBOLD and CHARLESTOWN

Written 15 February 2001

Fundamental needs of humanity do not change though sometimes, through arrogance, we think we have all the answers.

BANNERS GATE

Peter Cutts (1937–)

When, in age, we seek the com-fort of a time gone by;___ when we rest in me-mo-ries yet fear the rea-son why;___ God, be pre-sent in the mys-tery of a whis - - pered sigh.

© 2002 Stainer & Bell Ltd for the world except USA and Canada

When we hanker after childhood,
yet our friends have gone;
when we need a parent's caring
simply to go on;
God, in tender loving kindness
hold us, make us strong.

When at last we face the slumber
of our final sleep;
when we rest within your compass,
trusted to your keep;
God, through dazzling, dancing star-shine,
catch us as we leap.

© 2002 Stainer & Bell Ltd

Metre: 8.5.8.5.8.5.

Written 9 February 2001

It would be good to be energetic in death, especially if life had shorn us of our faculties and mobility! Resurrection, perhaps?

As constant as the pulsar's pulse,
as certain as the rising sun;
in darkness love will never die,
nor horror snuff out human worth.

The sounding of a baby's cry
as suckling, taken from her breast,
demands a mother's full concern,
so you have heard our hoarse lament.

Our cry goes out through all the world,
through this and each succeeding age;
your glance returns our wanting gaze,
and none escape your light or love.

© 2002 Stainer & Bell Ltd

Metre: LM

Suggested Tunes: ST BARTHOLOMEW and HEREFORD

Written March 2001

Written on Holocaust Day 2001. The love of God is as constant as the movements of the cosmos. Nothing, however heinous, can eradicate such love.

Amid this time of joy and expectation
that speaks of hope for here and all the earth;
such cosmic praise, a mighty acclamation
will herald here and now Messiah's birth.

God comes, a human child, amidst our laughter,
God comes to challenge all our fault and fear;
to meet us here in triumph or disaster,
the Saviour speaks but will we dare to hear?

This healing Christ, through birth and dereliction,
has called us to participate in care;
has entered human hell and degradation
and calls the world to love, to hold, to share.

© 2001 Stainer & Bell Ltd

Metre: 11.10.11.10. Iambic

Suggested Tune: INTERCESSOR

Written 3 April 2001

In the birth of a child the incarnation presents a challenge to the world, which can be lost as much through cultured praise as through popular sentimentality. This text was first sung at the Christmas Local Preachers' meeting (2001) in the Orrell and Lamberhead Green Methodist Circuit.

Gethsemane: temptation's empty stage.
Christ knelt and prayed and pleaded then, his crisis came of age.
The cup was taken, yes, the deepest draught.
The followers fell, betrayed it seemed, and Satan sighed and laughed.

The harrying hoard drew nearer to the place
where love and fear had had their fling, where anguish showed its face.
The darkness flamed as torches filled the night.
Air echoed to the thud of feet. They'd offer no respite.

The coldest kiss pressed in the evening's chill
against the face of one who'd loved; who'd loved and meant no ill.
A dance was joined by each man on that night.
A sad pavane would suit a king; what step the other's plight?

The shade of fear was glancing in Christ's eyes;
as Judas sensed the consequence his wealth would realise.
Each danced to death's discordant spring and chime,
of Hades' writhing dissonance, of resurrection's rhyme.

The sounds, the echoes, hanging in the air
rang out a solemn threnody, rang out with dull despair.
Gethsemane, the final curtain fell:
as Christ was taken through the night, while Judas glimpsed his hell.

© 2002 Stainer & Bell Ltd

Metre: 10 14.10 14.

Written 23 April 2001

Many years ago I wrote an unpublished text beginning with the word 'Gethsemane'. Starting from the same point, this hymn uses theatrical metaphors and consciously reflects Fred Pratt Green's 'Jesus in the olive grove'.

CONGLETON

attrib. Michael Wise (c. 1648–87)
arranged Peter Cutts (1937–)

Geth - se - ma - ne: temp - ta - tion's emp - ty stage.

Christ knelt and prayed and plead - ed then, his cri - sis came of age.

The cup was tak - en, yes, the deep - est draught. The follow - ers

fell, be - trayed it seemed, and Sa - tan sighed and laughed.

Arrangement © 2002 Stainer & Bell Ltd for the world except USA and Canada

WINDY CITY   *Peter Cutts (1937–)*

Ev-ery day life makes less sense as hope is dam-aged, faith is tried. We search for mean-ing, seek for strength, our cries are spurned, our needs de - nied.

© 2002 Stainer & Bell Ltd for the world except USA and Canada

Every day life makes less sense
as hope is damaged, faith is tried.
We search for meaning, seek for strength,
our cries are spurned, our needs denied.

Every day we question more,
we change our attitude of mind,
as things we thought were safe, secure,
are shaken, rattled, undermined.

Every day we stagger on,
each day our doubt a greater load,
each day less certain of the way;
God, shed some light upon this road.

© 2002 Stainer & Bell Ltd

Metre: 7.8.8.8.

Written 3 May 2001

A reflection written after the death of June Parker, a family friend.

108 From atoms to planets eternity changes

KEMEZA   *Peter Cutts (1937–)*

From at-oms to plan-ets e-ter-ni-ty chan-ges; the hues and the
co-lours that cov-er the earth, through sea-sons and cy-cles, the
world re-ar-rang-es, but sure is the love that has brought us to birth.

© 2002 Stainer & Bell Ltd for the world except USA and Canada

The wind and the weather distort vegetation,
the breakers are pounding and shaping the shore.
Our lives are spun round as each grief re-determines
the things that are doubtful and those that are sure.

Amid all this turmoil, this change and mutation,
the strained intertwining of living and strife,
one thing remains constant, relentless, determined:
that God goes on loving in death as through life.

© 2002 Stainer & Bell Ltd

Metre: 12.11.12.11.

Written 8 May 2001

The story of the kidnapping and murder of the son of the American aviator Charles Lindberg inspired this hymn.

To bring a city to its sense,
a nation to its knees,
they welcomed Nazareth's carpenter,
waved palms cut from the trees.

Hosannas filled the quiet air,
they strained to glimpse a view;
'Messiah' they acclaimed this man
whom Pharisees would sue.

He turned the tables upside down,
he spun their world around,
he challenged preconceived ideas,
flung hatred to the ground.

This man had learnt too much, it seemed,
knew ways of right and wrong,
his ear attuned to righteousness
sensed discord in their song.

The politicians and the priests
were threatened by this choice;
the hypocrites would silence him,
and still we shun his voice.

© 2002 Stainer & Bell Ltd

Metre: CM

Suggested Tunes: FINGAL and DETROIT

Written 5 May 2001

A hymn for Palm Sunday.

One world is fin
you have your plac
Before our God we c
none greater here, nor

You have your place and I ha
a way of faith we find or trace.
The final goal we may not know,
the path may change, may shift or ,oll.

I have my place and you have yours,
no one need win, this is no race.
And now that's clear, give me your hand
and let us walk devoid of fear.

© 2002 Stainer & Bell Ltd

Metre: LM

Suggested Tunes: OMBERSLEY and KEDRON

Written 12 May 2001

This text was written as a reflection on the observation that globalisation invariably results in the powerful impressing their values and political structures on the weak. Dialogue can result in mutual respect that will allow for different systems and cultures to exist side by side without threatening one another. The structure of the hymn is experimental, for me, using internal rhymes.

From season to season, through death and re-birth,
this world, through its phases, shows love has no dearth.
Such love is for sharing, to do good to all,
to nurture well-being, to echo God's call.

Through sensitive reason we fathom the need
of neighbours, of nature; we subjugate greed.
We offer each other the kiss of God's peace,
embracing earth's harmony, hatred will cease.

Through summer and autumn, through winter's release,
we welcome spring's coming with nature's increase.
All praise for the gifting of harvest and life,
all power to the ending of all human strife.

© 2002 Stainer & Bell Ltd

Metre: 11 11.11 11.

Suggested Tunes: DATCHET and FOUNDATION

Written 15 May 2001

A monotheistic reflection on Pagan cycles of the year. I use the term 'Pagan' with respect for ancient religious beliefs and practices which pre-date Christianity and not to imply atheism. I am grateful to my late son Jonathan and his friends for opening my eyes to this tradition.

We speak with eloquence and pride,
so sure of what is right and wrong,
determining another's fate,
while malice tunes our song.

Our human laws must not deceive,
for vengeance by its covert force
will neither comfort, nor relieve
our hatred at its source.

The justice God in Christ has shown
brings mercy to each hopeless case,
its task to chasten, then restore
each life through love and grace.

The questions that we ought to ask,
too painful for us each to bear,
are 'when?' 'to whom?' or 'how?' or 'where?'
we held back love or care.

And then, confronted by Christ's gaze,
admitting to the truth at last,
we'll learn forgiveness, gently loose
the stones we would have cast.

© 2002 Stainer & Bell Ltd

Metre: 8.8.8.6.

Suggested Tunes: ISLEWORTH and MISERICORDIA

Written 24 June 2001

I do not believe that capital punishment is ever right or acceptable. It enables us to reap vengeance rather than administer justice, however heinous the crime for which a person has been convicted. That Timothy McVeigh killed many people is not denied. Killing him made us no better. This text is offered in his memory and the memory of all who have been killed as a consequence of judicial process.

MERE   Ian Sharp (1943–)

Let us ce-le-brate this life, sing thanks to God for liv-ing; all cre-a-tion's gift and prize re-mem-bered in the giv-ing.

© 2002 Stainer & Bell Ltd

Let us celebrate this life,
sing thanks to God for living;
all creation's gift and prize
remembered in the giving.

Herons plough a silent sky
as fish below are skimming,
willows dip their silvering fronds
while sinking sunlight's dimming.

Autumn's day is auburn now
as Winter broods in waiting;
death, had hovered in the wings,
its prey anticipating.

Buried in the welcoming earth
as love, life's hold, releases:
now we celebrate our friend,
the surging torrent eases.

© 2002 Stainer & Bell Ltd

Metre: 7.7.7.7.

Written 30 May 2001

I live near to one of the Cheshire meres (a mere is a small lake). My father-in-law and many members of my wife's family are buried in a local churchyard overlooking two meres. The text grew out of a reflection on these associations.

It makes a banquet from a meal
when fellowship is shared with friends,
the tête-à-tête is blessed by God,
our food and conversation blends.

The little café where we meet,
the welcome hubbub that we hear,
the sights and smells that bring delight
are signs that God and love are near.

On special days we eat in style,
we celebrate with food and wine,
we meet with joy, give thanks and sing
to God of harvest, fruit and vine.

Yet every time we take a meal
the fact that we are being fed
confirms that God has heard our prayer:
'give us, each day, our daily bread'.

© 2002 Stainer & Bell Ltd

Metre: LM

Suggested Tunes: WILLIAMS and CORNISH

Written 29 June 2001

The Rev. Bob Davies, a Methodist Minister in Buxton, asked for a hymn about ordinary food – a 'café hymn'.

115   Noble, yet mystical, ground of creation

Noble, yet mystical, ground of creation,
star-fire and sun shower, and darkness and dreams;
all that through senses draws forth adoration,
God, we would worship, the love that redeems.

Human, yet awesome, the Christ, our relation,
offers a spirit: we learn to forgive.
Conquering our will this divine annexation
offers a way for us simply to live.

Spirit of living gives hope for our dying,
something transcending this life and its frame,
onward and upward in faith we are flying,
goal of existence, your love is our aim.

© 2002 Stainer & Bell Ltd

Metre: 11.10.11.10. Dactylic

Suggested Tunes: STEWARDSHIP and WAS LEBET

Written 10 July 2001

A hymn of the Trinity. Valerie Ruddle's tune 'Stewardship' is particularly fitting for the last verse.

What would God make of this building,
house of eloquence and praise,
God who walked the earth before us,
Christ of Galilean days?

He who left a home and family,
had nowhere to rest his head,
cast his lot with those derided
framed his life with what he said.

He who built a human temple
with the ones he sought to lead,
fended off each great temptation:
born of human power and greed.

Would he choose a place, more simple,
less ornate, of greater use,
where the hungry and the homeless
could be healed of their abuse?

If we follow in his footsteps
then this place must come to be
open to the poor, the homeless
where the richest grace is free;

Where our hope will glaze for glory
windows looking on the world,
where the broken will be welcome,
where love's given, never sold.

© 2001 Stainer & Bell Ltd

Metre: 8.7.8.7. Trochaic

Suggested Tunes: GOTT DES HIMMELS and RATHBUN

Written 23 July 2001

Verses 1, 2, 3, 5 and 6 of this text were written for my last service at Kingsleigh Methodist Church on 29 July 2001, and adapted from a text inspired by Wesley's Chapel, City Road, London, where I attended the Memorial Celebration for Fred Pratt Green on 9 June 2001. I love aesthetic beauty, and am surprised to find a Puritan streak in my character. The original final verses were as follows:

Let us choose a place, more simple,
less ornate, of greater use,
where the hungry and the homeless
will be healed of their abuse.

Here our hope will glaze for glory
windows looking on the world,
here the broken will be welcome,
where love's given, never sold.

The first of these stanzas, slightly re-cast, has now been interpolated as verse 4.

Troubled by joy, for our history has scarred us,
left us a remnant with tatters of faith;
yet we are hopeful for love still surrounds us
seen in the patterns of life that we trace.

Patterns that wind from the past to our present,
twisted and stretched, yet unbroken, held taut;
here God has found us where death and disaster
wrested assurance, where fear filled each thought.

Strong is the faithfulness God's care has shown us,
binding the broken and tending the frail;
shallow our faithfulness till love confounds us,
changing our vision, now hope will not fail.

© 2001 Stainer & Bell Ltd

Metre: 11.10.11.10. Dactylic

Suggested Tunes: STEWARDSHIP and WAS LEBET

Written 25 July 2001

Written for my last service at Bickershaw Methodist Church on 22 July 2001. Joy is a difficult concept for many to accommodate in the light of their experience. 'Challenged by doubt' is an accepted alternative to 'Troubled by joy' in the first line.

When we're loving one another,
not with sentiment and show,
but by sharing pain and hardship
Christ-like love will root and grow.

Let our loving spread yet further,
out beyond this present place,
reaching neighbours, friends and family,
compass all within God's grace.

Let us love in word and action,
may our sense of care amaze
those abandoned and rejected.
Love is not a passing phase.

© 2001 Stainer & Bell Ltd

Metre: 8.7.8.7. Trochaic

Suggested Tunes: SUSSEX and STUTTGART

Written 25 July 2001

Written for my last service at Westleigh Methodist Church, on 5 August 2001.

Here where harmony and music,
now when culture's highest art,
set the standard for our worship,
make us one in mind and heart.

Here where skill and presentation
sometimes mask much needed love,
bring us back to our beginnings:
close to you as hand in glove.

Here where intellect and freedom
seek in worship to explore
what it means to praise the God-head,
help us love our neighbours more.

Here are many gifts and graces
that experience has wrought
but, as you evoke our praises,
humble us, inspire our thought.

© 2001 Stainer & Bell Ltd

Metre: 8.7.8.7. Trochaic

Suggested Tunes: LAUS DEO (REDHEAD 46) and FOR THE BREAD

Written 31 July 2001

Written for my last service at Culcheth Methodist Church, on 5 August 2001.

In darkness we traverse the rock,
we find no cleft to hide in.
We look for God, whose voice is quiet,
for someone to confide in.

Where is the faith that, mixed with doubt,
can underpin foundations,
that forms the footings that will stand
our grief's adjudications?

The ledge of time on which we walk*
can lead our lives to glory,
yet often we misunderstand
as we compute our story.

O let us simplify the search,
look at this globe with reason;
then, in the world, not out of it,
seek comfort for this season.

Then as the darkness closes in,
while mist is curling round us,
at last, when all our hope is gone,
we'll find that God has found us.

* 'ledge of time' from *Summoned by Bells* by John Betjeman, p.88

© 2002 Stainer & Bell Ltd

Metre: 8.7.8.7. Iambic

Suggested Tune: ST COLUMBA

Written 30 August 2001

If there is no love and compassion here, nor hope or joy, then talk of after-life is pretty pointless. Often conversation about faith avoids doubt, yet this is an essential component in our understanding of life.

Let us all immerse in glory
simple lives God counts of worth,
magnifying sense and story,
all that God has given birth.
Feel the joy that sends us reeling
through the pulsing light of space,
sends us through cascades of feeling
losing all within God's grace.

Over heels each head is turning
looking for a reason why,
here in this ecstatic drumming
glory echoes to our cry.
Through our praise and in our singing,
in our prayers, and filling thought,
through the universe is winging
worship that our God has wrought.

© 2002 Stainer & Bell Ltd

Metre: 8.7.8.7.D.

Suggested Tune: AUSTRIA

Written 1 September 2001

'Kick of joy', a phrase used by the author Jeanette Winterson in a radio interview was the starting point for this text. Such a kick can send us reeling. From this the text developed.

122 God's on our side and God will grieve

© 2002 Stainer & Bell Ltd

BASIE

John R. Kleinheksel Sr (1938–)

God's on our side and God will grieve at car-nage, loss and death; for Je-sus wept, and we will weep, with ev-ery griev-ing breath.

God's on our side and God will grieve
at carnage, loss and death;
for Jesus wept, and we will weep,
with every grieving breath.

God's on their side, the enemy,
the ones we would despise;
God quench our vengeance, still our pride,
don't let our anger rise.

God's on each side, God loves us all,
and through our hurt and pain
God shares the anguish, nail scarred hands
reach out – love must remain.

God show us how to reconcile
each difference and fear,
that we might learn to love again
and dry the other's tear.

© 2001 Stainer & Bell Ltd

Metre: CM

Written 12 September 2001

This text has been chosen by the Hymn Society in the United States and Canada for publication in a collection to commemorate the destruction of the World Trade Center in New York on 11 September 2001. It was written within twenty-four hours of the events of that day, and already I had sensed that vengeance would soon be discussed and I wanted a vehicle to express my belief that God is not partial. The text was picked up by many congregations for local use around this time, both in the United Kingdom and the USA, and was also translated into Welsh. It was also published in 'Worship Live' No. 22, with 'Amazing Grace' as the suggested tune.

COLESDANE   *Peter Slade (1951–)*

The goal of our craft_ is to_ of-fer God_ praise,_ through rhy-thm or rhyme,_ by me-mor-able_ phrase. Un-leash-ing your_ skill, the Spi-rit will pro-vide the drift of your words, or the tune they will_ ride._ The drift_ of your words, or the tune they will ride.

The music we play, the songs that are sung,
the words that we write, their cadence or run,
the art and the craft, the gift God has given:
for these we give praise, give glory to heaven.

Words © 2001 and Music © 2002 Stainer & Bell Ltd

Metre: Irregular

Written 14 September 2001

Written at the request of Peter Slade for a hymn for the Methodist Church Music Society to celebrate the skills of its members, and set to a tune that he had already written. The hymn was sung at the meeting of the Society in the autumn of 2001.

124   Funny how in time of need

JENS

Nicholas Williams (1959–)

Fun - ny how in time of need we turn our thought to prayer,

talk - ing to the God we doubt so sure that some - one's there. so.

© 2002 Stainer & Bell Ltd

Funny how in time of need
we turn our thought to prayer,
talking to the God we doubt
so sure that someone's there.

Funny how when need is gone
we turn away again,
glad that all is going well,
our loss transformed to gain.

Funny, that inconstancy,
that fickleness we show;
stranger still, in spite of all,
that God should love us so.

© 2002 Stainer & Bell Ltd

Metre: 7.6.7.6. Iambic

Written 15 September 2001

I hope these words will not be mistaken for criticism. Following the destruction of the World Trade Center in New York, I became aware of the perverse nature and inconsistency of my own prayer.

The year goes turning round
but hate and spite still live.
How can we greet the foreigner,
the one that God will give?

Is fear the only force
that motivates our show,
or must we cleanse, eradicate,
the ones we do not know?

The image of one God:
endows a common face,
and though we come out differently
we live within that grace.

So let us vow to make
a time of love and peace,
when strangers will be welcome here
and selfish striving cease.

© 2002 Stainer & Bell Ltd

Metre: SM

Suggested Tunes: DONCASTER and DENNIS

Written 16 September 2001

On hearing the Chief Rabbi, Jonathan Sachs, speaking on the eve of Rosh Hashanah, the Jewish New Year, 2001.

And now, O God, what lies ahead
of hope or trepidation?
Help me to trust that you will bring
renewal, re-creation.

The love that brought my life to birth
has nurtured and protected
my being through succeeding years,
beyond all I expected.

That life that you have given me
has had its joy and sorrow.
Sometimes the past has seemed the best
and I have feared tomorrow.

And so I turn to you again,
as all around is spinning.
I greet the future, yet unknown:
make this a new beginning.

© 2002 Stainer & Bell Ltd

Metre: 8.7.8.7. Iambic

Suggested Tunes: DOMINUS REGIT ME and ST COLUMBA

Written 18 September 2001

Written for the retirement of my wife, Jackie.

127 Love is yours in the child you're bringing

MELODY SUNSHINE

Andrew Pratt (1948–)

Love is yours in the child you're
faith, born of God's in -

bring - ing.___ God is her be - gin - ning, God will
sis - tence,___ cry - ing out through all the world with

be her end.___ Round and round in the dance we're shar -
child - like joy.___ Fol - low now those foot - steps hewn from laugh -

- ing fun and joy and laugh - ter for a new found friend.
- ter danc - ing, leap - ing with a love we can't des - troy!

danc - ing, leap - ing with a love we can't des - troy!

FINE

Love is yours in the child you're bringing.
God is her beginning, God will be her end.
Round and round in the dance we're sharing
fun and joy and laughter for a new found friend.

This, your child, is a new creation,
born to face the future with a new found hope.
She is yours, for you to shape and nurture,
filling her with love, with strength to live and cope.

Share your faith, born of God's insistence,
crying out through all the world with childlike joy.
Follow now those footsteps hewn from laughter
dancing, leaping with a love we can't destroy!

Words and Music © 2002 Stainer & Bell Ltd

Metre: 9.11.9.11.

Written 22 September 2001

Written on 24 August 2001 in anticipation for Melody Sunshine, my great niece, who was born on 19 September 2001. Revised following her birth.

Tiny hands and tousled hair,
lungs that gasp for gulps of air:
as we hold you in our arms
child-like innocence disarms.

Star of darkness come to earth,
child of joy we hymn your birth,
child of hope for you we pray,
light up this and every day.

Caught within a wisp of time,
all our reason, all our rhyme,
fathoms depths of unknown scope,
depths of love and human hope.

O what happiness we feel,
and this happiness is real!
God inspire each faltering phrase,
for this child sing out with praise!

© 2002 Stainer & Bell Ltd

Metre: 7 7.7 7.

Suggested Tunes: SIMPLICITY (SONG 13) and INNOCENTS

Written 20 September 2001

Written for Melody Sunshine, my great niece, born 11.00pm on 19 September 2001. Sung during her baptism service at Trinity Methodist Church, Leyton, London on 14 April 2002. By this time we knew what her hair was like, so the first line was amended – 'Tiny hands and wisps of hair'!

Paradise unravels, chaos is the norm;
dissonance and anguish multiply the storm.
Life has lost its meaning, love is drained of force;
present dislocation hides, obscures, our course.

God forgive our blindness, show us where to start.
Offer us direction, Christ, our route and chart;
answer our confusion, blunt our hurtful hate,
open hearts to kindness, come, and not be late.

© 2002 Stainer & Bell Ltd

Metre: 11 11.11 11.

Suggested Tune: AU CLAIR DE LA LUNE

Written 8 October 2001

In 'Worship Live' No. 21, Janet Wootton wrote that 'at its worst, much of human history seems to be the systematic and horrific unravelling of paradise.' This text was written within twenty-four hours of the bombing of Kabul, Afghanistan, by the American air force.

OCEANPORT

John R. Kleinheksel Sr (1938–)

Be - yond the si - lence, still in grief, we ne - ver will de - sist____ from

crad - ling all that we re - call, for we re - mem - ber____ this:

three thou - sand lives are dead, not gone, and thou - sands more re - main,____ to

sing in - spired by hurt and loss as mem - ory quar - ries____ pain.

© 2002 Stainer & Bell Ltd

Beyond the silence, still in grief,
we never will desist
from cradling all that we recall,
for we remember this:
three thousand lives are dead, not gone,
and thousands more remain,
to sing inspired by hurt and loss
as memory quarries pain.

With agony that speaks of love
that we can never voice,
we share a unity of grief,
in this we have no choice.
Together we are bound as one,
for others do not know
our sense of grief, remorse, regret:
together we will grow.

Hold hands my friends, let's face the sun,
another new day dawns.
We never will forget their love
nor quench the tears loss spawns.
The future opens faster now
than we fear to tread,
let's build on love, and live in hope,
to meet what lies ahead.

© 2001 Stainer & Bell Ltd

Metre: DCM

Written October 2001

After 11 September – where next?

I offered these words which were posted on the website of the Hymn Society in the United States and Canada. They were accompanied by this preamble:

> *After the towers had fallen the silence was eerie. We have moved beyond this. We cradle memories like we would cradle a body, given the chance. Perhaps we hug ourselves as we imagine intimacy.*

> *While the dead are dead they are never gone. We are beginning to live with that knowledge.*

> *Only those who have lost as you have lost have any sense of what you have experienced and what you feel. There's no choice in this. These are the people who understand, who share your agony. These are the people with whom you find you can join hands, grow and find a way forward. The world greets you all too quickly, but together you can face it, though sometimes your progress will be so slow you will seem to stand still. Sometimes you will still cry out in sorrow, anger, pain. But you will go forward.*

That has been my experience.

In November, John R. Kleinheksel Sr responded: 'I came upon your fine text in the Hymn Society web page. The text captures a needed aspect of the grief that will be experienced for a long, long time in our country. Just last Saturday, I officiated at a graveside service for a 41-year-old father of two children, one aged two years, and a baby that was born to his widow eight days after his death in the World Trade Center attack. There is such sadness in the East Coast here, and around the country.'

When terrorism scars our lives,
in spite of calls to peace;
when governments are callous, deaf,
and, warring, will not cease
forgetting that the world we share
is only ours on lease;

When innocence and charity
are lost in seamless flame,
when bodies strew our empty streets
and law enforcers maim;
what can we do to wash away
the horror and the shame?

For where is God? And can we hear
the still, small voice of calm,
above the din and dissidence,
the cries of our alarm?
And can we ever risk the loss
of face to end this harm?

O give us strength to realise
the love we saw you live
when, in the name of Jesus Christ,
you suffered to forgive
the ones who sought to take your life.
God, show us how to give.

© 2002 Stainer & Bell Ltd

Metre: 8.6.8.6.8.6.

Suggested Tune: REVERE (John R. Kleinheksel Sr) *(see page 8)*

Written 25 October 2001

Another text arising from the events of 11 September 2001.

Was it a stable or a stall
began the history of us all;
incarnate from a woman's womb,
God, destined for a human tomb?
Was it a woman touched by love
as grace became her, like a glove?
She sensed compassion for a while,
astounded by Christ's fearless style.

Was it the signature of fate,
an action trivial or great,
when kissed within the olive grove
it tasted bitter as a clove?
That tree on which a Saviour broke
undignified, no English oak,
set at the crossing of our ways
set out the goal for all our days.

And now we see the Son arisen
no longer held within life's prison
no longer captive, crucified
he is not dead, though he has died.
The stable and the stall are gone
but still the story lingers on.
Was it the shepherd or the flock
who proved the greater stumbling block?

Far greater yet than birth or death
is love, God's singular bequest;
its fire must flame through every time,
to thaw each heart's resistant rime.
Ours is the charge to keep the faith,
in this and every waiting place,
to work with all our sense and breath
to be obedient unto death.

© 2002 Stainer & Bell Ltd

Metre: DLM

Suggested Tunes: SWEET HOUR OF PRAYER and SWEET HOUR

Written 10 November 2001

What was the starting point for Christianity – a birth, the actions of Jesus, his betrayal, his death or his resurrection? And what then?

The bricks and mortar of our lives,
the roof that crowned our greater thought,
will still define the path we tread
when grief assails what love has wrought.

Unmothered, yet not motherless,
but blinded by the tears we cry
we wander, wonder what will come,
and still we grieve, and still we sigh.

This strange coincidence of fate
that leaves us reeling in its wake,
we'll never fathom, understand,
as for your balm we reach and wait.

For all the mysteries of this life,
the riddle of this present death,
are more than we can understand;
God, give us peace in our distress.

© 2002 Stainer & Bell Ltd

Metre: LM

Suggested Tunes: OMBERSLEY and HAMBURG

Written 15 December 2001

By coincidence, my friend Damian Boddy, who chose the tunes suggested for this hymn, witnessed the demolition of the house in which he had been born and brought up, on the same day that his mother Elinor died. This hymn was written for him.

Reckless extravagance, laughter and daring,
lavish exuberance, thunder and light;
burning compassion and love, un-exhausted,
pouring from God with all passion and might.

Artist, explorer, composer and scholar
fathom the wonder of being and need,
piercing the mystery of love and creation,
take us where hope and existence would lead.

Searching the future, yet held in the present,
cradled by all that has brought us to birth,
here we should open our hearts to our neighbours,
loving with passion, for all we are worth.

Life is not wasted when lived for the other,
self-sacrificial, devoid of all fear.
Life is enhanced by intemperate giving,
giving that's gracious, unlimited, dear.

© 2002 Stainer & Bell Ltd

Metre: 11.10.11.10. Dactylic

Suggested Tunes: QUEDLINBURG and WAS LEBET

Written 7 January 2002

Artists, explorers, composers, scholars and many others push at the boundaries and open up the possibility of a window into the ground of our being. In response there is self-giving and sometimes ultimate sacrifice.

Elijah's cavern: simmering air,
a blustered headland, fractured rock,
a still, small voice, that counters fear,
while conscience reels in after-shock:
God's knows that trouble will ensue,
yet challenges the prophet's view.

We tread where saints have tramped before.
Across the ages faith has flown.
And now, within this present span,
by spirit gently, fiercely, blown
we meet the challenge of this day
or, maybe, simply turn away.

How easy to convince ourselves
that what we're doing now is right,
expedient and sensible,
all other paths we put from sight;
but still we hear the inner voice
and, like Elijah, make our choice.

© 2002 Stainer & Bell Ltd

Metre: 8.8.8.8.8 8.

Written 29 January 2002

Suggested Tunes: RYBURN and VATER UNSER

People of every generation have met challenges and made choices, like Elijah, who returned a changed man to face the problems from which he had hidden in the mountains.

Index of First Lines with Tunes

Of the following suggestions for music, the first in each pair is made from a hymnal familiar to readers in the United Kingdom, the second from an American standard work. Many of the tunes can be found in sources additional to those cited. Nos. 39, 47, 48, 50, 51 and 56 were first published in *Sound Bytes* (Stainer & Bell, 1999).

The following abbreviations are used in the index:

CHY   *Church Hymnary (Third Edition)* (Oxford University Press, 1973)
CP   *Common Praise* (Hymns Ancient & Modern Ltd/The Canterbury Press, 2000)
HP   *Hymns and Psalms* (Methodist Publishing House, 1983)
RS   *Rejoice and Sing* (United Reformed Church/Oxford University Press, 1991)
ST   *Salvation Army Tune Book* (Salvationist Publishing and Supplies Ltd, 1987)

CH   *The Celebration Hymnal* (Word Music/Integrity Music, 1997)
CVH   *The Covenant Hymnal* (Covenant Publications, 1996)
PH   *Psalter Hymnal* (CRC Publications, 1987)
TH   *The Hymnal 1982* (The Church Hymnal Corporation, 1982)
UMH   *The United Methodist Hymnal* (The United Methodist Publishing House, 1989)
WC   *The Worshiping Church* (Hope Publishing Company, 1990)
WR   *Worship & Rejoice* (Hope Publishing Company, 2001)

First lines of choruses are shown in italics.

Index of Metres

Index of Themes

(Biblical characters in *italic* type)

terrorism 35, 122, 129,
  131
Thomas 44
tide 23
time 11
towers 2
trance 67
Transfiguration, Mount
  of 20
Trinity 115
unemployment 82, 83

unity 38
vacuum 22
vengeance 112, 122
victim 13
vision 117
visions 34
void 22
war 57, 64, 74, 122, 129
watchmen 33
welcome 91, 125
wept 21

wilderness 25, 81
wisdom 19, 64, 98
woman taken in
  adultery 132
wonder 10, 18, 20, 26,
  30, 41, 43, 70, 89, 99,
  134
wonders 34
World Trade Center 122,
  124, 129, 130, 131
xenophobia 125

Index of Biblical References

Genesis 1 3, 10, 11, 18,
  23, 48, 57
Genesis 1:1–2 41
Genesis 1:1 – 3:24 98
Genesis 1:3 56
Genesis 1:3–5 6, 25
Genesis 8:22 108, 111
Genesis 11:1–8 2
Genesis 11:1–9 38
Genesis 17 – 50 47
Genesis 22:18 77
Genesis 45:7 117

Exodus 2 – 40 47
Exodus 3:1–6 58
Exodus 3:14 10, 39
Exodus 12:1–51 39
Exodus 13:21 – 14:25 25
Exodus 22:21 100, 125
Exodus 23:9 100, 125

Leviticus 19:10 100, 125
Leviticus 19:33–34 100,
  125
Leviticus 23:22 100, 125
Leviticus 24:22 100, 125
Leviticus 25:10–54 45
Leviticus 25:35 100, 125
Leviticus 27:17–24 45

Numbers 15:14–16 100,
  125
Numbers 35:25–32 112
Numbers 36:4 45

Deuteronomy 23:7 100,
  125
Deuteronomy 24:14–21
  100, 125
Deuteronomy 31:8 86

Joshua 47

1 Samuel 1:20–22 127
1 Samuel 2:4 97
1 Samuel 9 – 30 47
1 Samuel 18:1–4 92
1 Samuel 20:17 92

2 Samuel 1 – 24 47

1 Kings 1 – 2:12 47
1 Kings 19 7
1 Kings 19:3–18 79, 87,
  120, 131, 135

Job 13, 69
Job 9:4 22
Job 12:12–13 22

Job 14:14 126
Job 28:12 10, 22, 102
Job 28:20 22
Job 32:13 22
Job 33:33 22
Job 36:26 10

Psalm 4:1 17, 59
Psalm 4:4 1
Psalm 5:2 107
Psalm 6:7 80
Psalm 12:1 107
Psalm 17 59
Psalm 17:6 17
Psalm 22 13, 17
Psalm 22:1 1, 2, 8, 59
Psalm 22:9 104
Psalm 23 3
Psalm 23:4 1
Psalm 28:2 13
Psalm 31:9 80
Psalm 37:6 30
Psalm 37:7 73
Psalm 39:12 17, 59
Psalm 46:10 1, 73
Psalm 51:17 99
Psalm 54:2 17, 59
Psalm 57:8 30
Psalm 57:10 46, 93, 126

163